MEMORIES

KINGSTON UPON

HULL

To Bill with love

Margot
xx

June 1998

TRUE NORTH BOOKS

DEAN CLOUGH

HALIFAX

WEST YORKSHIRE

HX3 5AX

TEL 01422 344344

THE PUBLISHERS WOULD LIKE TO THANK THE FOLLOWING COMPANIES FOR SUPPORTING THE PRODUCTION OF THIS BOOK

MAIN SPONSOR
KINGSTON COMMUNICATIONS LIMITED

ADM COCOA (HULL) LIMITED

JF APPELBE AND COMPANY LIMITED

ARCO LIMITED

BRITISH AEROSPACE LIMITED

E BROWN & SONS (HAULAGE) LIMITED

B. COOKE AND SON LIMITED

EYMS GROUP LIMITED

JH FENNER & COMPANY LIMITED

OSWALD T HALL LIMITED

THE HEALTH SCHEME

HULL COLLEGE

HULL UNIVERSITY

HUMBER ELECTRICAL ENGINEERING COMPANY LIMITED

KINGS TOWN GROUP

WM. JACKSON & SON PLC

GEORGE LODGE & SONS LIMITED

MEREDITH BUSINESS EQUIPMENT CENTRE

MORCO PRODUCTS LIMITED

CB NORTH LIMITED

NORTHERN FOODS

ROBINSON & SAWDON LIMITED

FR SCOTT LIMITED

AC SKELTON & SONS LIMITED

WL THOMPSON LIMITED

UNIVERSITY OF LINCOLNSHIRE AND HUMBERSIDE

Donald Innes, 1908 - 1971

Many of the photographs within this book were taken by the late Donald Innes (left). The publishers would, therefore, like to thank David Innes, Julie Withell and Steve Betts of Innes Photographers.

Donald Innes opened his studio in Hessle during the Second World War. He was a cheerful ex-patriot Welshman who spent his career as a freelance photojournalist and photographer. Each of his pictures involves everyday life in Hull and the surrounding area, and has a special story attached to it. They provide a unique memory of life in Hull during the 50s and 60s.

These memorable images may be purchased in monochrome or sepia from Innes Photographers, 11-13 The Square, Hessle, East Yorkshire HU13 0AF. Tel: 01482 649271. The publishers would also like to thank Geoff Laws, Judy Laws and Margot Green.

Introduction

Welcome to *Memories of Hull,* a look back on some of the places, events and people in the city which have shaped the lives of local people over a period of around half a century. The following pages are brought to life by a selection of images from the not-too-distant past, chosen according to their ability to rekindle fond memories of days gone by and show how people used to shop, work and play in the area where they grew up. Modern image reproduction techniques have enabled us to present these pictures in a way rarely seen before, and the lively design and informative text has attempted to set the book apart from some of the other works available.

An early 1950s view of Victoria Square.

© INNES PHOTOGRAPHERS, 01482 649271

The chosen period is one which generally contains events within the memory of a large number of people in Hull - this is not a book about crinolines or bowler-hats! Neither is *Memories of Hull* a work of local history in the normal sense of the term. It has far more to do with entertainment than serious study, but we hope you will agree it is none the worse for that. It is hoped that the following pages will prompt readers own memories of Hull from days gone by - and we are always delighted to hear from people who can add to the information contained in the captions so that we can enhance future editions of the book.

Many local companies and organisations have allowed us to study their archives and include their history - and fascinating reading it makes too. The present-day guardians of the firms concerned are proud of their products, the achievements of their people and the hard work of their forefathers whose efforts created these long established organisations in the first place. We are pleased to play our part by making it possible for them to share their history with a wider audience.

When we began compiling *Memories of Hull* several months ago we anticipated that the task would be a pleasurable one, but our expectations were greatly surpassed. There is a growing appetite for all things 'nostalgic' and we are pleased to have played a small part in swelling the number of images and associated information available to the growing number of enthusiasts.

There is much talk in modern times about the regeneration of the local economy, the influx of new industries and the challenge of attracting new enterprise from other regions to Hull. And quite right too. We could, however, make the mistake of thinking that the changes are all happening *now,* but the reality is that there have always been major developments going on in the city. 'Change' is relentless and the photographs on the pages in the book serve to remind us of some of them.

Memories of Hull has been a pleasure to compile, we sincerely hope you enjoy reading it.

Happy memories!

Contents

Events and occasions

Left and above: Her Majesty the Queen visited the area in 1954 for a short private engagement at Sledmere Hall near Beverley. Sledmere Hall, the home of the Sykes family, is noted for the extensive collection of outstanding paintings and photographs, as well as the Sledmere Stud. This photograph shows Her Majesty as she was about to leave the Leconfield Airstrip after the three day visit.

It was taken in the last days of July 1954. She was accompanied by Group Captain A.F. Shelford. A few months earlier Her Majesty had completed a successful tour of the Commonwealth with the Duke of Edinburgh. As a point of interest, 1954 was also the year that Roger Bannister ran the first *four minute mile,* and *The Lord of the Rings* by J.R.R Tolkien was published.

The honour of opening the new Littlewoods store fell to the Lord Mayor of Hull, Alderman Fox J.P. on Friday 25th November 1955 at 11.00 p.m. Customers would have been tempted by the advertisements in the window describing the Christmas goods on offer in the weeks running up to the festive season, including a wide range of gifts for men for under £1.00. Understandably, most of the people featured here are women and it is interesting to see that full, long coats were

fashionable at this time and it was still more 'respectable' to wear a hat than not to. By modern standards the amount of store advertising for the Christmas period is very modest (and sensible), with only a couple of posters and a scanty

Christmas tree (in the right hand window) giving us a clue as to what time of year it was. These days we barely have time to unwrap our Easter eggs before the big retailers begin to bombard us with their Christmas adverts!

Left: *This publicity photograph was taken in 1951 - around half a century ago. The fun-loving young people shown here would, at the time of writing, now be of retirement age. The young ladies were all members of the Tivoli Theatre (Paragon Street) chorus line. Two lucky young men are also pictured, providing support and encouragement for their female friends. We know that the picture was taken in the King George Dock and it is likely that it would have marked the start of some new show or other and a valiant attempt at drumming up some new customers for the theatre. Sadly the theatre closed about three years after this scene was recorded. It was pulled down in 1957.*

Below: *University Rag Week in 1949. The proceedings look good-humoured enough as one would expect of an open-air gathering dating from half a century ago. Without doubt, Britain in general was experiencing a difficult times despite the high hopes for post-war prosperity. By September it was deemed necessary to devalue the Pound by 30%, such was the depth of the economic crisis. Brighter news was the end of clothes and sweets rationing in February 1949. On the literary front, the year saw the publication of George Orwell's classic 1984. During July, the month that this picture was taken, Britain's first jet airliner, the De Havilland Comet, made its maiden flight.*

"THE ROYAL PARTY SAW THE UNLOADING OF THE TRAWLER *PRINCESS ELIZABETH*, WATCHED BY CHEERING CROWDS"

Left and below: Her Majesty the Queen and the Duke of Edinburgh are featured in this picture from May 1957. The royal party had arrived at Paragon Station at 10.00 a.m before travelling to St. Andrew's Dock where they are seen in this picture. The party saw the unloading of the trawler *Princess Elizabeth* watched by cheering crowds before moving on to the University via Cottingham Road. A visit to King George Dock and to the Hull Royal Infirmary were also included on the unusually busy itinerary which took over 6 hours, involved meeting 200 people and travelling 23 miles along the city's roads. The royal party left the city on the Royal Barge which departed from Corporation Pier at Nelson Street at 4.27 p.m.

Left: The Queen's visit to St. Andrew's Dock in Hull is featured here in a picture taken to mark the occasion in the late 1950s. Her Majesty was accompanied by the Lord Mayor of Hull and Mr. H.L Hopkins, as well as Lord Middleton the Lord Lieutenant of Hull and the East Riding.

Below: Looking as radiant as ever, Her Majesty the Queen visited Hull in June 1967 to open the new Hull Royal Infirmary. A medical 'guard of honour,' formed by white-gloved nursing staff, can be seen lined up on the right of the photograph, as the Queen, accompanied by the Lord Lieutenant of East Yorkshire, Lord Middleton approaches the hospital. Hull was proud of the new hospital which was constructed on the site of the old Western General Hospital and staffed by a dedicated team of 700 health professionals. Still on a medical theme, 1967 saw the world's first heart transplant operation in South Africa, and the passing of the Abortion Bill in Britain.

> **"HULL ROYAL INFIRMARY WAS BUILT ON THE SITE OF THE OLD WESTERN GENERAL HOSPITAL"**

Below: November 1953 in the Oxford Street/Eleanor's Terrace area near Wincolmlee. There wasn't much to smile about after the heavy flooding which occurred when the River Hull burst her banks. These youngsters are making the most of things, floating a couple of oil drums along the street as the flood waters recede. It wasn't much fun for their parents though, these were the days before it was commonplace for most ordinary people to have insurance against the effects of flooding, and it would take weeks before their simple possessions would be dried out and their lives returned to normal.

Right: As thoughts turned to Christmas, in November 1954, there was widespread misery in the Witham and Old Town areas when a massive high tide caused serious flooding in the communities. This picture from the time shows the floodwaters after the worst of the them had already begun to recede, though the shop keeper still found it comforting to have a stout board across the entrance to her little businesses to keep the lapping water at bay. Various posters beneath the newsagent' shop window can be seen for publications as diverse as the Hull Daily Mail, the Picture Post and Woman's Weekly. Wall's banana flavoured ice cream, Airman Cigarettes and Anglo chewing gum were also on offer from the little shop.

Above: A moment to treasure. The memory of this brief encounter would have been etched on the mind of this young fan for the rest of her days. The ever-youthful Cliff Richard played in a concert at the town in January 1960. As we see, he was rather more accessible to his supporters than he is today, though he doesn't *look* much older! Still on a romantic theme, 1960 was the year that Princess Margaret married Antony Armstrong-Jones after succeeding in keeping their courtship private. The announcement was made just one week after the birth of the Queen's second son, Prince Andrew.

Left: Thanks but no thanks... is the unspoken but very clear message here. The young lady on the right was having no success, despite her coy look and carefully curled hair, in persuading the elegant visitor to handle the freshly-caught fish as a group of bemused workers look on. And no wonder! Piles of kits are stacked up in the background, ready to be filled with the fruits of the latest expedition. The scene was captured along the St. Andrew's Fish Dock, the heart of Hull's on-shore fishing industry.

August 1965 and a picture taken to record queues of young people outside the Tower Cinema, eager to see the new Beatles feature film "Help!" The delightful old building first opened its doors to the public in 1914 and many Hull folk will have happy memories of exciting dates with their future partners at the Tower. The cinema in general was extremely popular in Hull, and at the time that the Tower opened, there were 29 establishments showing silent movies in the area. Talking pictures arrived in Hull, as in the rest of the country, in 1929.

Kingston Communications - the Hull telephone people

Kingston Communications has a unique heritage within the City of Hull. It is a company whose history and experience stretches back to the very beginnings of telecommunications in Britain. Famous far and wide as the land of cream telephone boxes and untimed local calls it is also a company moving forward, enhancing new opportunities and technologies to deliver advanced products and services to its customers.

Today Kingston remains resolutely independent, based on deep-seated municipal roots going back to the turn of the century. At that time, local authorities were given the power to establish their own telephone networks to compete with the US owned National Telephone Company.

The NTC had established itself very quickly in the rapidly expanding urban areas of Britain, and the Postmaster General, whose own Post Office network was struggling for customers, saw locally-controlled alternative networks as a viable competitive alternative. Several local corporations took their chance - six in total.

Telephones had already come a long way in the 25 or so years since the first one was invented by Edinburgh-born Alexander Graham Bell. Telephones were first used over short distances between two fixed points, but later a group of telephone wires were brought to a central board

*Top right: The first NTC directory from 1896, incorporated into the Corporation network in 1911. **Above:** A switchboard operator outside the old Kirkella Exchange. **Right:** Boy switchboard operators, 1880. Boys were employed initially but their 'skylarking' led to girls taking over.*

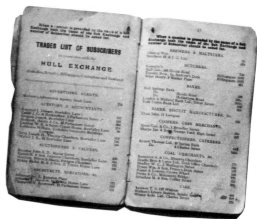

connected to more distant stations. Initially boys were used to relay messages orally between subscribers. An early document describes how the preference for boys rather than women was soon reversed. "In the first exchanges boys were generally engaged as operators, but due to their inquisitive spirits, mischievous behaviour etc. they did not give their best attention and girls began to replace boys in this role." Switches were soon introduced so that the subscribers could talk to each other direct. These switches gave rise to the term 'switchboard', the first one being introduced in London in 1879. Before the invention of the telephone the main means of long distance communication was the Telegraph. As telephone use became more widespread the Post Office realised that the new method of communication was a serious threat to its nationalised Telegraph Service. In 1880 the High Court ruled that no public telephone system could be operated without a licence from the Postmaster General. A private company provided a telephone service in Hull at around this time. It later amalgamated with others and became the National Telephone Company.

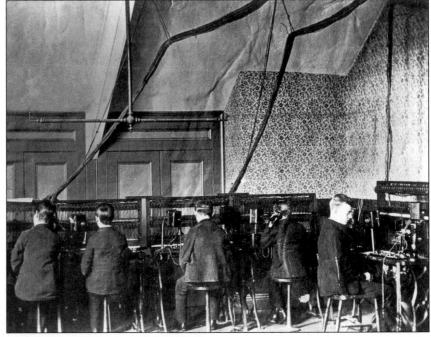

telephones and consult two directories. In November 1904 the Corporation, having received its licence and sanction to borrow over £40,000 for the purchase of plant, opened its first exchange in the Trippett Baths building in Wincolmlee. The Ericsson Bell switchboard was equipped to serve 2,000 subscribers from 20 manual positions. Approximately 200 miles of wire were used and there were a quarter of a million soldered joints within it. A manager, Mr T. Holme, who had already acted in a similar capacity for Portsmouth's telephone service, was appointed at a salary of £200 per year. By 1911 the Post Office Network had attracted only 50 customers. Hull Corporation had 3,000 and NTC some 9,000. Competition was intensifying.

Services came and went as various acts of Parliament and Postmaster Generals attempted to determine exactly what was acceptable and desirable in a public telephone service.

By 1895 the National Telephone Company was serving 742 subscribers from their Bowlalley Lane property, while only 52 Hull subscribers favoured the system operated by the Post Office.

1903

We've been making Telecommunication Equipment since then . . .

Ericsson
TELEPHONES LTD.

22 LINCOLN'S INN FIELDS : LONDON W.C.2
Tel: HOLborn 6196   Works: BEESTON, NOTTS

KEEPING IN TOUCH

Aided by the
KINGSTON UPON-HULL CORPORATION TELEPHONE DEPARTMENT

GOLDEN JUBILEE 1904 - 1954

The Only Municipal Telephone Undertaking in the United Kingdom

In the same year, a decision was made which was to establish Hull's independence for years to come. The Postmaster General had taken steps to secure a UK monopoly of telephone services, buying out the NTC and many of the local authority owned services which had fallen foul of poor planning or commercial failure. He made Hull's bid for a new licence conditional on the purchase of the NTC network in the city-at a cost of £192,423. The council approved the purchase and the sole municipally-owned telephone company survived and prospered.

However, in 1898 a Select Committee of the House of Commons favoured a system with local telephone systems in competition with the National company. It prevailed and the 1899 Telegraph Act allowed municipalities to borrow money to set up their own systems under licence from the Postmaster General. Out of 1334 authorities only six, with Hull proudly amongst them, eventually set up telephone services. More legislative activity followed and Hull Corporation gained its licence on 8th August 1902, provided it kept to the same exchange area as the National company covered. There were some snags in the system, for example having to rent two

Right: A manual exchange in service from 1924 to 1956. Centre: The cover, and an advert from the 1954 brochure celebrating the company's Golden Jubilee.Top: An old exchange switchroom circa 1899.

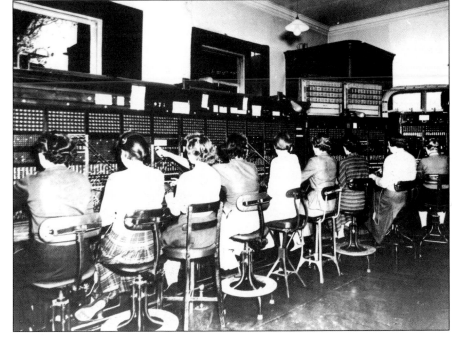

lishments. Some remain, but are now converted to automatic operation.

In the earliest years of the House Exchanges the job of a telephonist was very different to what it is in modern times. Margaret Dukes lived to be 102 and recalled, when she was in her 80s, her experiences at her exchange when she attended a staff re-union in 1984. On joining *Telephones* the young ladies would be issued with two aprons. A white apron was to be worn while operating the *boards,* and a black one for cleaning the House Exchange and black-leading the fireplaces! An early directory from the time that Margaret Dukes had started with the company has an interesting listing. It shows that the Police and Fire Brigade could be contacted by dialling 467, but a cautionary note beneath the listing states "Fire Brigade not yet connected."

In the years which followed, a network of House Exchanges was set up around the area to cater for the increasing number of subscribers. Typically these were converted houses which contained the telephone exchange and staff necessary to serve specific areas. At their peak there were 14 such estab-

The bombing raids during the Second World War were a real test for the staff. Several of the exchanges were hit but everyone pulled together to keep the service going, even though at the height of the disruption, after one particularly heavy raid, there

was only one remaining line out of the city to Leeds! After a bombing raid the *Telephones* staff would turn up at the nearest exchange and volunteer to do whatever was necessary to maintain the service. Members of the company would perform miracles to keep it operational. In May 1941 part of the administrative offices at Mytongate was destroyed by a bomb. About 80 switchboards and 2,000 hand sets were completely ruined. The most serious damage was that caused to underground cables by the bombs and the efforts of the repair teams were often hampered by the blackout. After one severe raid 5,000 subscribers were cut off after several cables were severed. During the conflict about 4000 lines were provided for the Services and these would always have top priority in the event of a fault developing.

Throughout the history of the company the ladies charged with supervising the House Exchanges were powerful characters. They would keep the girls on their toes with wide responsibilities ranging from making sure that each call was answered within *20 seconds* to limiting the amount of coal used to heat the working area! One former telephonist recalled a particularly stern supervisor who 'never missed a trick' and would require a written explanation if an operator made even the most minor mistake. "We knew she had a heart of gold though, and we could always tell if one of the girls was pregnant because the same supervisor would carry the girl's chair for her when she had to work in a different part of the exchange.

Of course, supervisors and staff would never call each other by their christian names, and the girls were not *officially* allowed to talk to each other while 'on the boards', in fact, they were not even supposed to look back over their shoulders in the early days when someone entered the room. "Instead we would would try to see the reflection of the person in the shiny bits of chromework on the boards in front of us."

*Above: A picture from September 1955 of two members of staff working on the switchboard at Guildhall. **Left:** Telephone House reception shortly after opening.*
***Facing page, top:** Listening to Teledisc in August 1957. **Facing page, bottom:** The Central Exchange, Mytongate, 1963.*

powerful illustration of just how much the world of telecommunications has changed in less than half a century.

Calls from ships were particularly welcome because they were sometimes accompanied by an invitation to an on-board cocktail party. Again, the supervisors would take an active interest even in the girls' social activities, and insist on chaperoning them when an invitation like this came along.

In the 1950s each House Exchange would keep 10 directories listing every subscriber to the system. As new subscribers joined the operators at each exchange had to carefully update the directories *by hand,* and at the end of the year these would be passed to the printers so that the new directories could be produced. The daily job of updating the directories could be very time consuming at times, though some of the girls regarded it as a welcome change from their other duties. The days of the old manual switchboards and call boxes are recalled by a recently retired lady operator. "Callers had to put two old pennies in the box for their 6 minute call" she said. "At the end of time allowed a bulb would light up on the switchboard and we would then interrupt the call by saying *'Your time is up, will you take another call?'* This was the only time that the operator was allowed to listen into a conversation, and people usually completed their call or put another twopence in the box. Our retired operator remembered how, in the early 1950s, a colleague had been monitoring a romantic couple for slightly longer than was strictly required. It was a compelling conversation and near the end of it the young man concerned said

The work could be demanding. Indeed, for many years there was a minimum height requirement in the company in recognition of the considerable amount of stretching necessary to connect all the calls. But there was an element of fun and enjoyment involved too. Friendships which began at the company often endured into retired life, and hundreds of couples met and married their partners while working there. Former telephonists will recall the 'ship to shore' service which described the operator-assisted connection between the exchange and ships, hotels, working mens' clubs....and some other establishments too. Basically these customers relied upon the operator to dial their numbers for them, and a closer relationship naturally developed between the operators and these clients. One operator who worked for the company in the 1950s told how the now massive Brough works of British Aerospace had only *two* lines, each working on the 'ship to shore' basis, for many years, a

"Anyway, I'm going to hang up now, I think the operator's still listening." "Oh no I'm not" replied the operator, before realising they could hear *her* ...and collapsing with embarrassment!

During the 1950s the Hull Corporation department introduced 'Golden Pages', the forerunner of 'Yellow Pages', for its golden jubilee classified advertising directory. The first recorded information services were also introduced during this period.

"ONE OF THE MANY SOURCES OF PRIDE AT THE COMPANY IS THE 'CALL FATHER CHRISTMAS' SERVICE WHICH BEGAN IN 1952"

One of the many tremendous sources of pride at the company is the 'Call Father Christmas' service which began in 1952 and could be reached by dialling Hull 211211. It was the first information service in the U.K and the concept has been copied by similar organisations throughout the world. The first year of the service attracted 20,000 callers, with 35,000 customers the following year. All paid 2d for the three minute compilation of story and music spread over three nightly installments. As the reputation of the service grew many calls were received from other parts of the country, and a considerable number were taken

from overseas. This was quite extraordinary at the time. Geoff Laws, the former *Telephones* Public Relations Officer, now retired, remembers writing many of the scripts for the service from 1962 onwards. His small team of volunteers would gather around a tape recorder, either in his home or in the basement of the Guildhall where each complete 3 minute episode would be recorded in one 'take' - there were no editing facilities in those days. If a mistake was made the whole thing had to recorded all over again, often taking hours to get 'just right', testing everyone's *Christmas spirit* to the limit! The recordings were made by volunteers who did the work in their own time, just for the pleasure of it. One year, as Christmas approached, Geoff was asked

Below: Recording the 'Call Father Christmas' broadcast in 1962. Pictured from left to right; Judy Laws, Colette Greenwood, Len Wharton, Margot Green, Geoff Laws and Jack Lloyd. **Facing page top:** *Installing Drum metering equipment in September 1964.*
Facing page bottom: *A demonstration taking place at Telephone House in October 1964.*

by a person at the Guildhall when the recording sessions were going to start. It turned out that staff at the hall always looked forward to the recordings because the sound travelled up to the higher floors through the central heating pipes!

1964 saw the passing of a major milestone with the construction of Telephone House, the new headquarters on Carr Lane, Hull. The foundations of the building rest on 576 piles driven 60 ft into the clay subsoil beneath it. The site was once the location of dozens of shops and houses, most of which were badly damaged or destroyed during the war. On opening the building boasted around 47,000 square feet on five floors. It had cost £550,000 to build and contained equipment worth slightly more than that amount in the form of the most up to date switching gear. The facility could cater for 12,400 subscribers with the ability to be extended to cater for 20,000.

Kingston Communications has 500 kiosks around its 120 square mile network area, 250 of these being K6s. A K6 is the classic Hull 'cream telephone box' which was introduced from 1936 and designed by Sir Giles Gilbert-Scott. Unlike BT's red kiosks, Hull's cream boxes do not have a crown symbol above the door. This is because the city's telephone service has always been independent of the Post Office (which ran the UK telephone service prior to the creation of BT in 1984). Six of these K6s are now listed buildings. K6s are manufactured from cast iron with

wooden doors. Kingston Communications has, wherever possible, a policy of preserving its unique cream kiosks. Those that are vandalised are broken down and used as spare parts to ensure the maximum number of them can be maintained. Kingston Communications also has a listed K1 kiosk, dating from the 1920s, in Hull's Market Hall, and a further preserved example within Telephone House.

The structure of Hull's telephone service continued its evolution when on February 17th 1987 the City Council announced plans for a Municipal Company to be formed. The City Council had in the past avoided constraints on local government capital spending by using 'leasing' to finance a large proportion of the Telephone Department's modernisation programme. Faced with the threat of legislation that could stop this method of financing and with subsequent adverse effects on the investment timetable, proposals gathered momentum for the creation of a municipal limited company. Other methods of raising finance would then become possible.

The complicated process of transforming the Telephone Department into a limited company became underway and on 7th December 1987 a new licence was issued by the Secretary of State, under the 1984 Telecommunications Act, to the council's wholly owned operating company, Kingston Communications (HULL) plc. This became effective from 1st January 1988.

Today, Hull's telephone system remains unique. Kingston Communications, as the former Hull Telephone Department operates one of Europe's most advanced telephone networks, serving some 170,000 customers across a 120 square mile network -

the same size as in 1904. Also unique is the company's pricing policy. It offers socially orientated tariffs which have resulted in one of the highest penetrations of telephone users in the UK, some 94% of households having access to a telephone.

The company also took a major step forward in the 1980s with the launch of the UK's first all-digital telephone network. The advantages of digital telecommunications; clearer calls, increased reliability, the opportunity to provide fully itemised bills and newer services, heralded a new era. From 1983 the Department embarked on a five-year modernisation programme aimed at major improvements in the telecommunications service and facilities provided in the Hull area. The invitation to tender attracted worldwide attention, with a long-term contract for the supply of System X equipment awarded to Plessey and GEC who won the initial contract.

The knowledge and experience Kingston has gained is much sought after. They provide consultancy services to large private system users and the emerging local cable TV franchise operations. They have representatives on national and international advisory bodies and are founder members of the European Group of locally-based telephone companies. The workforce have a depth and breadth of expertise unmatched in the industry.

The way forward
During the last decade Kingston has diversified its business. The company's overall strategy has been to grow businesses around its core telecommunications expertise while maintaining a heavy investment programme in its own public network.

Kingston believes that the quality of network management is crucial to being able to give the customer what he or she wants. They know that customer care will become ever more vital as the market place becomes increasingly competitive. Such issues as network integrity, the ability to change quickly to meet customer demand and future-proof solutions will become absolutely fundamental to the company's success. Kingston is investing in new-generation technology to create the high speed network needed to deliver variable bandwidth services.

The Kingston portfolio of services will grow rapidly to meet the demands of the business and local community. Video-on-demand, the growth of video-conferencing and the requirements of the business community for data services will drive forward Kingston's strategy in this area. The company will achieve these aims by continued investment, driving down the costs of delivering services and continuing to offer a socially orientated policy of low-cost access to its network and services.

The Kingston Communications Group is diverse but dynamic. Each of the eight businesses is focused completely on its own customers, whilst at the same time enjoying the synergies which come from in-depth Group-wide expertise. The individual businesses within the Group encompass network operations (including fixed wire, broadband and satellite), software development, communications equipment testing, sales and maintenance, directory publishing and internet service provision. All its operations are rooted in a deep understanding of communications technologies and its customers' needs.

Kingston Communications is a growing global operator. From its core network in the city of Hull, the Group has grown into an international business. The "Hull Telephone Story" has certainly been an interesting read over the last century. We look forward to the next chapter with interest.

Top: Celebrations in 1984. **Facing page bottom:** *A new Telephone Corporation van in 1958.* **Facing page top:** *One of Kingston's famous cream telephone kiosks.*

Around the city centre

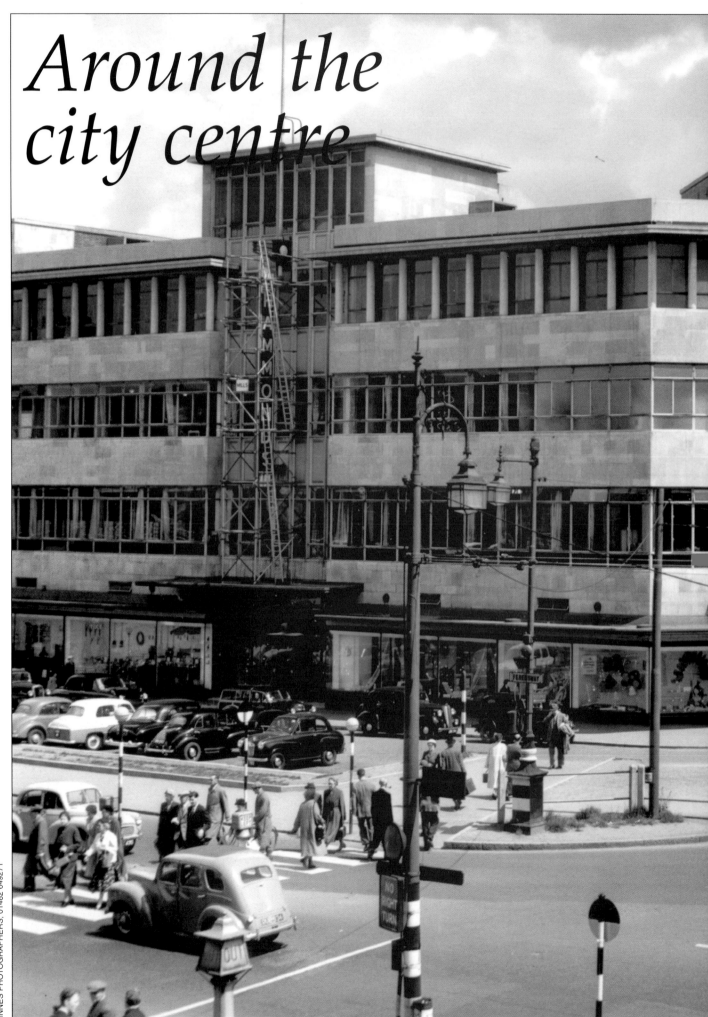

Hull's best-known department store, Hammonds, captured in a picture from June 1956. By this time the store had been open for just six years and was part of the rebuilding process which occurred in Hull after the war. This was the second Hammonds store to be built on the site, the original store being destroyed by enemy bombs in the war. The business was originally started in 1821. Jameson Street can be seen to the right of the picture and Ferensway, with the zebra crossing, leads off to the left. Belisha Beacons are present on the crossing, they took their name from the Minister of Transport, Mr. Hore Belisha, at the time of the 1930 Road Transport Act.

Right: The imposing architecture of the buildings around Victoria Square in a scene dominated by the City Hall and the Dock Offices. The photograph was taken in 1953 and we can see from the clock on the Docks Offices that it was approaching noon. Construction work began on the City Hall in 1903 and the building was completed about seven years later. Interestingly, the Dock Offices are of much earlier origin, being completed and opened in 1871. Their significance was recognised when they were designated a Grade II listed building. they were taken into the ownership of Hull City Council in the late 1960s and were later put to good use as the home of the City's Maritime Museum. The forecourt of the City Hall is the location of the statue of Queen Victoria. In the distance the Queen's House development can be seen. It had been open for just two years when this picture was taken.

Below: This elevated view of the City Hall and Queen Victoria Square dates from 1952. The imposing building which was Hull's City Hall was constructed between 1903 and 1909. The statue of Queen Victoria marked the location of the underground public lavatories. The statue was unveiled by the Prince of Wales in May 1903, long before the creation of the public conveniences. Overhead power cables for the trolley buses of the public transport system can be clearly seen in the photograph. Modern buildings in Paragon Street, on the right of the picture, housed up-to-date offices and shops, including Hepworth's in the new triangular-shaped block. Carr Lane is shown on the left of the photograph.

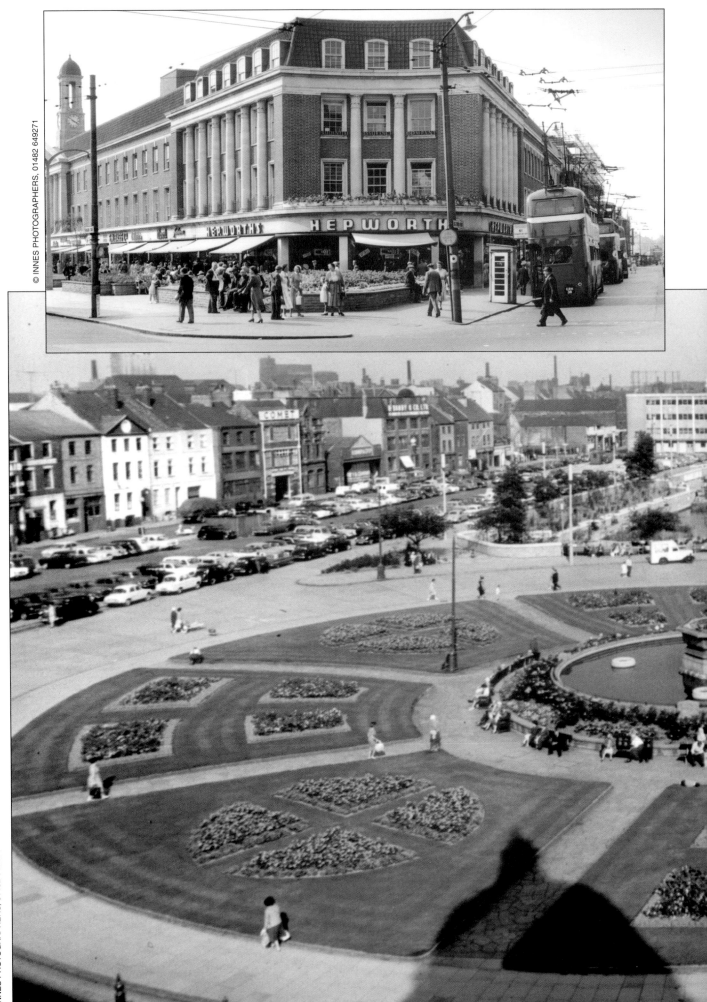

Left: We can be irritatingly precise about the origin of this photograph. It was taken at 3.50 p.m on August 23 1955 and the main subject of the town centre scene is the relatively new, triangular-shaped Queen's House development. The neo-Georgian style of the building was considered to be rather advanced when it opened in 1951. The modernity of the building contrasts sharply with the queue of trolley buses parked at the right hand side of the picture. Many people mourned the passing of the trolleybus era which began in 1937 and ended in 1964.

Below: Shoppers take advantage of the seating in Queens Gardens to enjoy the warm September sunshine in 1961. The carefully laid-out flower beds and extensive lawned areas in the heart of Hull provide a welcome oasis of tranquillity where students, workers, shoppers and visitors can enjoy liberal helpings of peace and quiet, away from the hustle and bustle of the rest of the city. The white walls of the Technical College can be seen in the distance, with the statue of William Wilberforce standing in front of it. The monument was rebuilt at this spot in 1935; it had originally been located between Prince's Dock and Queen's Dock when it was built in 1834.

Below: Ferensway, the broad expanse of roadway in the heart of Hull, as it appeared on a busy day during October 1955. The Hammonds department store can just be seen on the left of the photograph and Hull's Cenotaph in Paragon Square. The cenotaph was unveiled in September 1924, constructed to commemorate the sacrifice made by the men of Kingston upon Hull in the First World War. The monument was built from Portland stone and inscribed with the words "Their Name Liveth Forever More." The clarity of the photograph belies the fact that it was taken almost half a century ago. The advertisements on the side of the buses for 'Oxo' , Will's Woodbines, Zopol, Cornelius Parish (the Austin dealership on Anlaby Road) all look as clear as ever. The taxi office is just in view on the right of the picture, suitably located for the convenience of passengers using the railway station.

HULL'S CENOTAPH WAS UNVEILED IN SEPTEMBER 1924 TO COMMEMORATE THE SACRIFICES MADE IN THE WAR

Above: The corner of Humber Street is featured in this picture from September 1955. This crowded scene records the activities which took place at Hull's wholesale fruit, vegetable and flower market. This was already a one-way street when this picture was taken. Several familiar business names are visible in the picture. On the right is Roberts and Almond, with R. Wrigglesworth and Son across the street. Note the interesting three-wheeled articulated truck on the right of the picture. These Scammel vehicles were favoured by British Railways because they were adept at manoeuvring around the tight confines of their stations and surrounding town centres. They were also put to good use in environments such as the one pictured here, where their tight turning circles could negotiate the many obstacles to be found here.

Left: *A mid-1950s view of King Edward Street is captured in this photograph. The broad street was once one of the busiest shopping areas in Hull. It was created after one of the improvement schemes at the turn of the century, at the same time as the construction of Jameson Street. The prominent large store on the junction of King Edward Street and Jameson Street was Dolcis. This valuable corner site was later rebuilt and redeveloped shortly after this picture was taken, but Dolcis remained at this location afterwards. The distinctive domed towers of the Dock Offices can be seen in the centre of the picture. The grand building was completed in 1871 and later provided a home for Hull's Whaling Museum and collection of maritime artifacts.*

Below: *A wealth of nostalgic feelings are evoked by this photograph. It was taken along George Street early in 1951. The Young People's Christian and Literary Institute can be seen on the right of the picture. Further along the street, on the right, it is possible to see the elaborate facade of the Criterion Cinema. The popular place of entertainment was once known as the Majestic, and had been built in 1915. It was famous for having shown some of the first primitive colour footage in Hull and later, in the 1920s, for having its own resident light orchestra. The establishment had been re-named Criterion in 1935 and it closed its doors on the public for the final time in 1969. The building was pulled down in 1973.*

Above: An elevated view of the Queen's House development in a photograph dating from 1966. The Chapel Street branch of Lloyds Bank dominates the foreground of the scene and, at the adjacent taxi rank, an old Austin and a much more typical Ford Zodiac taxi can be seen waiting hopefully for their fares. The *Zodiac* was a 1960s icon in many ways, made famous and desirable by the 'Z-cars' television series. In the distance it is just possible to make out the Yorkshire Bank and two of the distinctive turrets of the Docks Offices. Events in 1966 were dominated by England's victory in football's World Cup competition. The economy was enjoying less success at this time and Harold Wilson's Labour government found it necessary to impose an unpopular wages freeze. This was also the year of the terrible Aberfan disaster in South Wales and the sensational trial and conviction of Myra Hindley and Ian Brady for the murder of three children.

Above right: The darkness of a cold November night was brought to life by these Christmas lights, thoughtfully positioned along Jameson Street. The annual switching-on ceremony was always covered in the local press and performed by a local dignitary or celebrity. At the time this picture was taken the Christmas lights had been been displayed each season for just three years. Of course, there was a commercial reason for the annual display, the idea being that shoppers would be attracted to the city shops from miles around. Several of those shops can be seen in the photograph; Loyds, Harry Jacobs, Lennards, Evans and Fletchers to name but a few.

Right: Late July 1966, and a lone car park attendant oversees the comings and goings at the small Hammonds car park. According to the clock on the Guinness sign opposite, the photograph was taken at 3.30 p.m. A variety of motorcars from the period adds colour to the scene. It is interesting to reflect upon the events which would have been on the minds of the passers-by shown here. The country as a whole was 'Swinging' to the tunes of the Beatles and the fashions of Mary Quant were taking the London fashion houses by storm. The spring general election saw Harold Wilson's Labour government returned with a majority of 90; they faced tough times with the economy and a growing industrial relations problems throughout the workforce.

Above left: The imposing, modern facade of Lloyds Bank in a photograph from 1956. It is striking to see just how bright and clean Chapel Street looks. Lloyds Bank and the other business premises depicted in this picture were, of course, all part of the Queen's House development which was completed in 1951. The era was one of significant retail development in Hull. The Hammonds store was constructed in 1950 after the original building had been destroyed by wartime firebombs. The city centre streets look much quieter in this picture, but certain parts of Hull were blighted by bottlenecks as serious as any found today. Notice the coach-built pram being pushed across the road on the left. This small-wheeled design had been popular for many years and well cared-for examples were passed around families almost endlessly.

Left: The bright, modern lines of the Hull Co-operative Society dominate this view of Jameson Street. The picture dates from August 1963. Readers may have visited the Skyline Ballroom and Restaurant which could be found on the top floor of the building. Sadly the Co-op ceased trading from this location but

part of the property was taken over by British Home Stores. It is pleasing to see the number 64 trolley bus approaching the zebra crossing, evidence of a cleaner mode of public transport in days gone by. The statue at the bottom right of the photograph was erected in honour of Andrew Marvell (1621-78) the famous Hull M.P and poet who had a close association with Oliver Cromwell around three centuries ago.

Above: The special offers at the opening of the new Littlewoods store in Hull caused queues around the building in November 1955. The traditional retail premises in this picture were along Whitefriargate, facing the bright, new Littlewoods store. Included among them were Boots, J. Lyons & Co. the grocers, the Kardomah Cafe and John Collier the gents' tailoring chain. The long queue shown here ran along Whitefriargate and across the road to the Littlewoods store. This was a time of considerable optimism after the depressing years of the Second World War. There was a tremendous amount of rebuilding work on the city, involving both commercial and residential property.

Below: This modern facade of Queen's House belies the fact that it was constructed in 1951. This picture was taken in June 1956 and features several well-known *high street* names along the parade of shops, including Weaver to Wearer (gents outfitters), Peter Lord, the Direct Raincoat Co., among others. In the distance two of the three towers of the Docks Offices can be seen and, beyond that, the dignified local headquarters of the Yorkshire Penny Bank. The scene was captured late in the afternoon on this sunny June day, and shoppers can be seen enjoying a welcome rest on one of the benches near the raised flower beds.

Above: Queen's Gardens and the surrounding area as it appeared in 1966. The modern building on the left houses the Customs and Excise offices. The Queen's Gardens area was created after the Queen's Dock was filled in during the 1930s. The dock had become unsuitable for the demands of modern shipping and the added inconvenience (for ships and local traffic) of the Monument Bridge, which had to be raised and lowered for entering vessels, made the future of the dock very limited. By 1935 it was decided to fill in the dock - a move seen as very bold at the time, and the splendid open gardens we love today were laid out on the site of the old dock. The job was considered complete when the statue of Hull's most famous son, William Wilberforce, was removed from its original site at the Wilberforce Bridge and rebuilt at the Queen's Gardens. That considerable undertaking was accomplished free of charge by a firm of local builders.

On the move

Above: *The war had ended some four years before this photograph was taken. The military men featured here were all R.A.F firefighters, complete with kit bags, waterproof clothing and shovels. The picture was taken in August 1949. We admit to being uncertain about the type of aircraft shown in the picture. Many Lancaster and Lincoln bombers were converted for troop carrying opera-* *tions after the war and it is possible that this was one of them.*

Inset: *This photograph was taken in October 1965. It features the unmistakable smooth lines of Sir Donald Campbell's Bluebird. This was the original car used to secure the land speed record by the irrepressible British*

hero and it was being displayed at Kenning's Analby Road motor showroom. In this picture we see that the cockpit lid had been propped up and a mirror positioned to allow enthusiasts to glimpse the controls. It is sad to remember that less than two years after this picture was taken Donald Campbell was to lose his life in another record attempt. This time he was attempting to capture

the record for the fastest speed recorded on water. The jet-powered Bluebird was an entirely different craft. It overturned at a speed of 300 m.p.h killing the 45 year-old Campbell outright when the plucky Englishman was within yards of beating his own water speed record of 276.33 m.p.h. The nation mourned the passing of one of its favourite sons and his

Above left: This picture dates from December 1957. It was taken to record the innovative advertising medium that was being used to promote the latest film at Hull's Cecil cinema. The 'cute' electric delivery vans were owned by British Railways and made local deliveries from the Paragon Station. They were advanced for their time, being almost silent in operation and, crucially, fume-free as they scurried around the streets of the city. The film being advertised was Robbery Under Arms, starring Peter Finch, Ronald Lewis, Maureen Swanson and a youthful David McCallum.

Left: This slightly elevated view across the rooftops has Paragon Railway Station as its central feature. The photograph was taken in July 1967. The railway station had existed since 1848 and was built to replace the Dock Green station which had opened

some eight years earlier but was too far away from the centre of Hull to be convenient for passengers. Dock Green survived as a goods-only station until 1961.

Above: The busy newspaper stand outside Paragon Station was the location for this 1951 photograph. The picture is clearly 'stunted-up' to promote the Sunday Chronicle's £1000 crossword competition. It would be difficult to believe that either of the smart gentlemen on the right of the scene were newsvendors - they look considerably better dressed than many men do on their wedding day! Other newspapers on sale include the *Reveille* (at 2d), the *Sunday Pictorial* and the *News of the World.* The advertising board behind the stand offers various excursions including a trip to York Races for just 8s 8d - or less than 45p in modern currency.

Above: Hessle Square with the new traffic islands under construction. The photograph was taken in August 1959. Modern road-builders might scoff at the way the heavy kerb stones have been laid out, almost like childrens' building bricks to mark the layout of the road. A variety of 1950s motor vehicles, including the East Yorkshire Transport double decker bus add tremendous character to the scene, and the warm summer sunshine rekindles happy memories of a time when life was enjoyed at a more comfortable pace.

Below: A vintage car rally in Hessle was enough to pack the roadside along the route when it took place in 1950. There is something slightly ironic here, for the older people watching the procession would have been looking at the old cars with a genuine sense of nostalgia, no doubt remembering the days when the spindly vehicles were a common sight on the roads in the area. Grandfathers would have been recounting the time when they saw the first motor car locally, and the first time they were lucky enough to travel in one, to the inquisitive youngsters enjoying this spectacle. Now, around fifty years on, we can take pleasure in a scene which is nostalgic for us, as we see local people from the past indulging in a few minutes of nostalgic recollection.

Above: September 1953, just eight years after the end of the Second World War, and a new more convenient way to shop was becoming a familiar sights on the roads around Hull. Home deliveries, with the traditional image of a grocer's boy panting around the neighbourhood with his bike laden with foodstuffs, was nothing new. But the idea of taking the shop to the shoppers was quite different and the idea found favour with hundreds of customers. We might smile at the design of the mobile shop as pictured here, with its high counter and row of tiny open windows on the roof, but in the days before every new estate had an adjacent convenience store or supermarket they were a *godsend* to the people who lived there.

Right: The Co-operative mobile shop was supposedly being loaded up before setting off on its rounds according to this picture. The cynics among us might be forgiven for thinking that this was merely another publicity photo, taken and distributed to make more people aware of the home delivery service being promoted by the grocery

supremos at the time. Whatever the reason behind the picture, it provides an interesting look back for the modern reader, not only at the world of shopping, but at the world of work too. The Co-op staff look very smart in their long white overalls, but the task of loading two trays of bacon looks rather labour intensive by today's standards!

Above right: Some may have thought that the Co-op had decided that a mobile shop should look like an ordinary shop with a wheel on each corner, and if that was the plan they certainly succeeded. Still, mobile shops were a great idea and it speaks volumes for the concept that modern times see every major retailer running trials with home delivery services. We were curious about the role of the smart gent with the note book putting a supervisory finger on the arm of the driver in this picture.
Was he a high-powered manager from Co-op H.Q checking up on his mobile shopkeeper - or a member of the *Grocery Police* on the lookout for contraband corned beef?

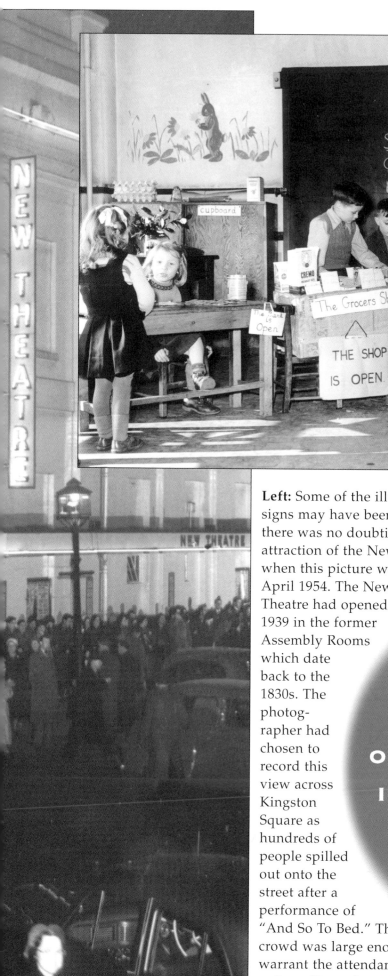

blackboard

Shopkeeper
Sweet Shop - Ian Saville Bridget
Grocer - Graham Michael
Bank - Nona

The Grocers Shop

THE SHOP IS OPEN

The bank is Open

cupboard

The Swee
This shop Open

Left: Some of the illuminated signs may have been faulty, but there was no doubting the attraction of the New Theatre when this picture was taken in April 1954. The New Theatre had opened in 1939 in the former Assembly Rooms which date back to the 1830s. The photographer had chosen to record this view across Kingston Square as hundreds of people spilled out onto the street after a performance of "And So To Bed." The crowd was large enough to warrant the attendance of a lone police officer - he can just be seen in the centre of the picture. The City Council bought the theatre in the early 1960s and invested heavily in extensive refurbishments in the mid-1980s.

Above: Pupils from Hessle's Penhurst County Primary School get to grips with the intricacies of the retail world, overseen by the watchful eyes of their teacher. The picture was taken in 1950, so the children shown here would be in their mid-50s at the time of writing. It is nice to see that the names of the children are written on the blackboard, leading to thoughts of "where are they now?"... and did *Nona* really end up working in a bank?

> "THE NEW THEATRE OPENED IN 1939 IN THE FORMER ASSEMBLY ROOMS"

Hundreds of people, mainly, but not exclusively women and children, can be seen enjoying some summer entertainment in East Park at the Bank Holiday Gala. The picture was taken late in August, in 1951. The fashions from the time are bound to bring back memories - and the clarity of the photograph belies the fact that it was taken around 50 years ago. Most of the ladies in the scene are wearing hats, and almost every one of the young boys has a smart jacket for the occasion.

Below: A familiar scene to anyone who visited Hull Fair in the 1950s. The little lads in the foreground appear to be finding it hard to choose which of the attractions to visit next, and who could blame them, with a sheer wall of sound, colour and movement confronting them from every angle. Amazingly the scene is around half a century old, and many readers will remember going to the fair as youngsters - or perhaps the first time our parents allowed us to visit the fair unaccompanied. The smells and sights remain with most of us well into adulthood. In the days before almost every youngster had a T.V and computer in his (or her) bedroom an outing to a fair would be a considerable treat.

Right: Long before the days of Alton Towers and similar theme parks, the role of providing mystery and excitement for thousands of youngsters from miles around was assumed by Hull Fair. This picture was taken during an uncharacteristically quiet period in 1956. The fairground was set up on a site in the Walton Street area and covered several acres, leading to the claim that it was one of the largest events of its type in Europe. The sights and sounds of the fairground - not to mention the distinctive aromas that wafted around the many attractions, would remain with visitors for the rest of their lives. The fairground itself had two distinct personalities; the character projected during the daytime was a powerful attraction to families with children. The excitement mounted as darkness fell, the noise level rose and the fair filled with teenagers seeking thrills and spills... and maybe more.

A lot of thought and preparation had gone into the construction of this stand at Hull fair. The stand belonged to G.A Padgett and Sons, the Cromwell Street ice cream specialists who had recently won first prize in a national ice cream competition held at Porthcawl in South Wales. We know from the advertising material seen here that the competition was held on October 11th 1956, and the photograph was taken just nine days after the firm's success there. Padgett's prices look very attractive

by today's standards. Cones and wafers cost 6d (less than 3p in modern currency) and the posters urged people to sample the award-winning products in Padgett's cafe or at the fairground. It is interesting to see the clothes being worn by the people in this picture. Some of the footwear looks quite inadequate for the soggy conditions - and most of the people featured have legs spattered with mud from the many puddles on the showground.

A scene from October 1955 looking across the the colourful tops of the attractions at Hull Fair. The area around Walton Street enjoyed a week of popularity every October, drawing thousands of visitors to it every year. On the right of the picture the apparently flimsy structure housing 'Sir Robert Fossets's Giant Circus' can be seen. Posters on the side of the tent advertise the presence of lions and tigers. Other attractions included the Steeple Chaser, the Shooting Rapids, Pat Collins' Miniature Racing Cars and the ubiquitous Waltzer.

This scene features a small corner of Hull Fair as it appeared in 1961. Small it may be, but it features virtually every element of the characteristics which attracted scores of thousands of eager visitors to the site. The crowds were certainly out in force when this scene was recorded. The helter-skelter on the left of the picture was operated by Billy Williams, according to the sign on the side of it which also invited mums and dads to take a ride with their children. Note the hot chestnut wagon on the right of the picture selling bags of freshly roasted nuts at sixpence a time. The photograph is dominated by the Big Wheel which could be seen for miles when lit up at night.

"THE BIG WHEEL
COULD BE SEEN FOR
MILES WHEN LIT UP
AT NIGHT"

Above: It was smiles all round in October 1950 when this moment was captured at Hull's fair. The well-dressed party were enjoying one of the exhilarating fairground rides when the photographer spotted them.

Down at the docks

Old Town and the Docks in a bird's-eye view from 1954. Note the Hull-New Holland Ferry in the foreground, slightly to the left of centre. It was 'made redundant' in 1981 with the opening of the Humber Bridge and was withdrawn from service. Another landmark is the distinctive outline of Holy Trinity Church dominating the Old Town area on the left of the photograph as it has done for hundreds of years. Beyond the splendour of Holy Trinity it is just possible to discern the spoked pattern of Queen's Gardens with the old Dock Offices beside them. The Central Police Station had been constructed in 1959 and the Customs House building and Telephone House were about to be opened when this picture was taken. The Central Library extension was completed two years before this scene was recorded, completing a series of post war construction projects which reshaped Hull after the devastating bombing.

Above left: This fascinating photograph was taken in March 1958. Those *in the know* will immediately recognise the location as being Hull's King George V Dock, and it would be impossible not to be impressed by the composition of the picture which has created a near three dimensional effect for the reader. The tugs in the foreground are the *Yorkshireman* and the *Rifleman*, and their vertical funnels and intricate rails and rigging make for a very appealing picture. Notice the railway wagons on the left of the scene ready to be loaded onto a ship for export. This Dock was known by some people as 'Joint Dock' because its initial construction in the early 1920s was undertaken as a joint venture between the North Eastern Railway and the Hull and Barnsley Railway.

Left: This photograph dates from the mid-1950s and features a busy shipping scene in the King George Dock. This was the last of the ten Hull docks to be opened when ships began using it in 1914. The King George Dock was constructed by the North Eastern Railway Company and the Hull and Barnsley Railway Company.

The oldest of the docks is Queens Dock which dates back as far as 1778. It closed finally in 1930. At the time this photograph was taken the docks in Hull were experiencing a time of prosperity and it was not uncommon for railway trains to queue in order to get onto the docks. Many of Hull's docks went into a period of decline in the 1960s but King George Dock was extended in 1969 to cope with the increasing volume of container cargo which began to go through it.

Above: Good news for British exports. A steady flow of motorcars, many for the American market, was also good news for the dock workers at the King George's Dock. This picture was taken in September 1950. Note that the cars are left hand drive for the export market. They can be seen here being raised in a heavy net by the giant cranes on the side of the dock. 1950 saw the opening of the Festival of Britain, on the South Bank of the Thames in London. It served, albeit temporarily, to lift some of the post-war economic gloom in the country. People from Hull, and from all over Britain, flocked to the exhibition which was opened by the King and Queen in May 1950.

Above: Around a dozen trawlers can be seen in this picture from 1949. The location was, of course, St. Andrew's Dock, and the vessels are waiting for the next tide before setting out to sea. At the time this picture was taken Hull's fishing industry was in fine shape, with around 150 vessels working from the port and an army of processing and distribution workers supporting them in the port. St. Andrew's Dock was opened in 1883 and was designed exclusively for the use of fishermen. In later years this fact was reflected in the dock being referred to as the *Fish Dock*. Later still, with the decline of Hull-based fishing operations, St. Andrew's Dock was closed and filled in. Leisure activities went on to reign, in the form of a multi-screen cinema and bowling alley, where the once-thriving fishing industry ruled.

Right: A very busy scene indeed at St. Andrew's Dock, the skyline being full of masts and rigging from the hardy trawlers moored along the quayside. Hull's first enclosed dock, the Queen's Dock was established over 200 years ago in 1778. The dock featured here was opened in 1883. Most, but by no means not all of the workforce involved with Hull's docks was drawn from East Hull, leading to thriving communities there with a common interest in all things nautical. The decline of port activities in the 1960s saw a reduction in trade and the closure of Town Docks. In the following decade the Victoria and St. Andrew's Docks suffered the same fate.

Left: This delightful picture is certain to rekindle nostalgic memories among local folk. It features St. Andrew's Dock and captures the hustle and bustle of a typical working day in the area with a crispness and atmosphere rarely seen in a photograph. The foreground is dominated by the corrugated rooftops of the bicycle sheds and the cluster of 1950s motor cars which are parked rather haphazardly beyond them on the quayside. This picture dates from the mid-1950s but the construction of the dock itself, by the Hull Dock Company, took place some 70 years or so before that time, in 1883. This was the heart of Hull's fishing industry for many years, providing employment for thousands of people over that time until the decline and eventual closure of the dock in 1975. After this time much of the activity relating to Hull's fishing industry was conducted by the adjacent Albert Dock.

Above left: It was a dismal day on the streets of Hull when this photograph was taken. And it wasn't just the wet weather that was putting the damper on things, for the photograph was taken to record the dock's strike which took place in 1954. Brighter news during the same year was the announcement that, at long last, all rationing in Britain was to come to an end, some *nine years* after the end of the war.

Above: This will be a familiar scene to anyone who worked at the Riverside Quay and Albert Dock. The scene was recorded in 1961, the dawn of the most dynamic decade in the second half of the century. At the time the picture was taken the new facilities along the distant south quayside had only been open for a short time. The articulated lorries look rather fragile in comparison to their modern equivalents - the vehicle piled high with sacks looks overloaded with just a single axle on the trailer. Interestingly, the public right of way along the River Humber was maintained, after the construction of the sheds on the left, by taking the footpath over the roof of the building - hence the modern black railings stretching out to the horizon.

A busy scene at the top end of the Iceland market, one of the two fish quays on the St. Andrew's Dock. This tremendous photograph dates from 1959 and shows a variety of workers involved with the fishing trade on the crowded quayside, surrounded by kits of fresh fish. St. Andrew's Dock first opened about a century ago, in 1897 and catered for the sale and distribution of fish throughout the lifetime of the industry in Hull.

Sporting life

Above: One of Hull City's stars of 1949 was Raich Carter, seen here doing a little solitary training to hone the ball control skills that Hull supporters appreciated so much. Carter had a successful career in football, both as a player and a manager. In later years he went on to play inside right for Sunderland and England, and also managed Hull, Leeds and Mansfield.

Left: A sea of faces, most sporting a friendly smile, look up to the photographer as the Humber Ferry approaches the Corporation Pier in October 1949. Most of those featured here were Grimsby Town supporters en-route to Boothferry Park for the Division Two local derby. The final scoreline was a 2-2 draw.

Above: This impressive picture shows the crowd waiting to enter Boothferry Park for the F.A Cup match against Manchester United in the 6th round of the competition. It dates from February 1949. The game was watched by a staggering, record gate of 55,019. Sadly Hull lost by a single goal to nil. It is interesting to see the signs indicating the price of a ticket for the match - 2/6 with 'no change given.' The photographer has cleverly managed to attract the attention of the waiting supporters before taking the shot, and the expressions on the faces of the orderly crowd make the scene fascinating for the modern reader.

Right: An historic moment in the development of Hull City, as Don Revie signs for the club in November 1949. Among the directors and officials attending the signing is Raich Carter, the club manager. Who could have guessed that Revie would go on to make such an enduring mark in his own right as a successful club manager and later as the manager of the national side? Raich Carter was 34 when he joined the Hull club after a 14 year stint with Sunderland. He rose to become player-manager but resigned in September 1951.

By December the same year he was recalled as the performance of the club plummeted towards the relegation zone. He ended his playing career in 1953.

Above right: Don Revie and Raich Carter pose for the camera shortly after Revie had signed for the club in 1949 for the considerable sum of £20,000. Revie had been with the (then) lowly Leicester club previously, having joined them in 1944. We cannot be certain, but the picture gives the impression that Raich Carter was in the process of taking his new young player to his digs - keen eyes may just be able to make out Revie's small suitcase in his left hand. The puddled-road and the small black Morris saloon paint a dreary picture of Don Revie's first impressions of his new club. How things have changed in the world of football! Revie left Hull in October 1951 to join Manchester City and later went on to play for Sunderland in the 1956 season. Two years later, in 1958, the move to Leeds was made marking the start of his long association with the Yorkshire club. Don Revie died in May 1989 after a long battle against motor neurone disease, a sad loss to the world of football.

Above: *This is a superb historic picture. It features Hull F.C's Wembley team in May 1959. The team faced Wigan in the final of the prestigious Challenge Cup competition. Thousands of fans travelled to London for the clash which took place in hot and humid conditions. The crowd of 80,000 saw an entertaining match which ended in a defeat for Hull by 13 points to 30. On their return to Hull the team attended a reception at the West End Hotel hosted by the Lord Mayor of Hull, the Sheriff and leading figures from the world of rugby.*

Right: *A clash with Manchester United has always been a massive crowd-puller at any football ground, and the chance to see one of England's most entertaining and successful teams in action against Hull City was grasped enthusiastically by local supporters. This picture demonstrates the lengths that fans were prepared to go in order to get a good view of the game. The photograph dates from February 1949. Apart from the obvious changes to safety regulations from that day to this, the trends in fashion have changed drastically. Most of the young men (who would, at the time of writing, now be in their seventies) look well-enough dressed to spend a day working in a bank with their smart turned-up trousers, shiny shoes and raincoats. They would be lucky to get away merely having their leg pulled if they arrived at a modern game looking so well-groomed.*

Above: Fun and games were the order of the day when this scene photograph was taken. The picture dates from April 1952 and shows the Hull R.LF.C Supporters Club's Boulevard Ragtime Band as they are about to set off on their coach."Up the Airlie Birds for the R.L Championship" proclaimed their banners. Other events from this year included the death of King George VI and the accession of Queen Elizabeth II, the death of the land speed record holder John Cobb on Loch Ness, and the testing of Britain's first Atom bomb. This was also the year that the block-busting feature film *Singin' in the Rain*, starring Gene Kelly was released.

Right: A rare moment of relaxation is captured in this picture from 1957, as members of Hull Rugby League team take a well-earned break from a training session at the Boulevard ground. the players look in relaxed mood as they sit on the straw bales in front of one of the stands. The advertising boards in the background promote the Hessle Road radio business known as Moss Radio Ltd. Events from 1957 include the launching, by the Soviet Union, of the world's first space satellite, followed soon afterwards by the first dog in orbit. It was also the year that the Queen made her first Christmas television broadcast and the government introduced Premium Bonds.

This well-ordered scene depicts crowds waiting at Boothferry Park in 1966. The much-awaited fixture took place between Hull City and Chelsea on April 1st. The solitary mounted policeman on his large white horse appears to have little to do here, you can't imaging the fans causing much trouble for him as they wait patiently to enter the ground. During the month that the picture was taken the Russians sent the first spacecraft to orbit the moon and Freddie Laker began his cut-price Atlantic airline service. Later, an unmanned American spacecraft actually landed on the moon and protests about the war in Vietnam reached new heights on the streets of central London.

dances. In the 1970s there was a return to popularity of the sport with racing at the Boulevard ground of Hull F.C.

Left: This marvellous action-shot dates from 1950 and features the match between Hull City and Tottenham Hotspur. The game was seen by a crowd of 38,345 and the match was won by Hull with a scoreline of 1-0. Hull's inside right, Fred Smith, scored the winning goal. Notice the absence of crowd barriers of any kind and the fact that the tightly-packed supporters are only a few feet from the touchline.

Top: Tension mounts at the start of a Speedway heat on a damp evening in April 1949. Speedway racing first began locally on a site at the old Hedon Airfield in 1948 and the Hull speedway team was known as the Vikings from these very early days. A railway halt was opened on the Withernsea line to accommodate the attending speedway fans at round this time. The speedway track at Hedon closed after only a few years due to falling atten-

Far left: The excitement and passion evoked by the clash between Hull City and Doncaster Rovers is recorded in this picture from around half a century ago. It was taken in early December, 1951, and features the popular hull City player Raich Carter as he returns to the dressing room after the gruelling match. He must have had a good game, judging by the elation shown on the face of the young lady fan in the foreground.

Above: Twelve members of Hull's intrepid Speedway Team line up for the camera in this photograph from half a century ago. The riders are posing at the trackside with a J.A.P-engined machine which looks rather similar to the bikes used today, with it's spartan construction, lack of brakes and rigid (i.e, unsprung) 'rear end.'

Above right: Gritty determination is evident on the face of Bob Baker as he slides into a left hand corner. The picture dates from 1949. Notice the exposed chains which transmitted the power from the engine to the clutch and on to the back wheel. We can only grimace at the thought of the damage they could do in the event of an accident.

Right: Two Speedway Aces flash past the camera in this 500cc duel from 1948. The machines are characteristically spartan in their equipment. The handlebar controls had merely a heavy clutch and a throttle controlling the powerful engine. There were no brakes or gears on the machines which were stripped down to the bare minimum weight in order to maximise acceleration and top speed.

> **"SPEEDWAY RACING FIRST BEGAN LOCALLY ON A SITE AT THE OLD HEDON AIRFIELD IN 1948"**

At work

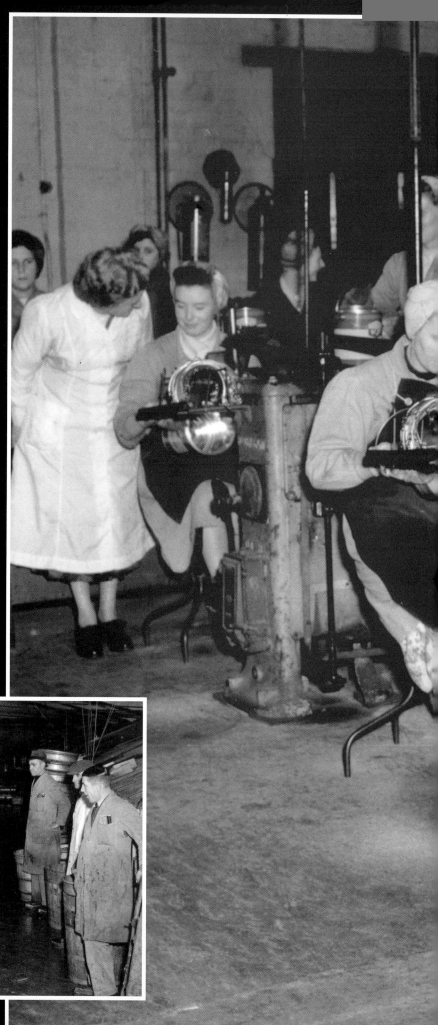

Right: These ladies worked at the Metal Box Company, for a long time one of the biggest manufacturing organisations in the country, when their picture was taken in 1956. The production line featured here was concerned with the assembly of paint tins; the ladies working on it are attaching the handles to the tins, overseen by a supervisor in her immaculate white overall. The work looks rather repetitive, but in 1950s Hull few people would have complained about that. The young lady nearest to the camera would probably have recently left school - her mind seems to have been miles away when the photographer released the shutter.

Below: The atmosphere in one of the processing sheds of the Hull Ice Company can be seen in this picture, taken in February 1961. You can almost smell the cold fishy air! The conditions for the workers were, to say the least, on the basic side, and the work was hard and repetitive. Fish would be cleaned on the long sturdy tables - and considerable care had to be taken when working with the sharp knives in the cold and wet conditions. From the Fish Dock the valuable foodstuff would be dispatched to towns and cities throughout Britain. Rail transport was the favoured method of distribution for many decades, being speedy, reliable and economical. The mid 1960s saw a change of distribution method in favour of lorries. This was due to the declining number of railway stations and the growth in Britain's motorway network.

Above: This stark 1950s scene shows around a dozen flat-backed lorries, most of them fully loaded with kits of fresh fish ready for transportation to nearby processing establishments. The picture is sure to bring back memories to the hundreds of people who worked at this location half a century ago. The trucks themselves have a nostalgic appearance which evokes memories of their whining gearboxes and axles as they struggled with their heavy loads around the quayside area. Of course, there was no power assisted steering in those days, and the drivers developed tremendous upper-body strength from their exertions in the draughty cabs. After the end of the war there was an influx of ex-War Department trucks on the market, and many of these tough machines saw service well into the 1960s.

Below: Half a dozen sturdy workhorses, complete with attendant staff in their smart white overalls, pose for the camera outside the Hull Brewery Company. The photograph was taken in 1957 and keen-eyed observers may just be able to make out the shape of a brewery tanker lorry behind the group, on the right of the picture. The four-legged gentle giants were a familiar sight on the roads around Hull for many decades but it was inevitable that one day they would be superseded by mechanical methods of beer distribution. That day came in the 1970s, much to the sadness of many local people who had enjoyed the sight of the heroic animals as they trundled silently from pub to pub.

THE HULL BREWERY CO. LTD.

The University of Hull: the legacy of 'a few local friends'

The Duke of York, (later H. M. King George VI), laid the foundation stone of the University College of Hull on 28th April 1928. The founder of the University College was Thomas Robinson Ferens who, in 1925, had given £250,000 to 'form a nucleus of a University College'. He consulted various academics then called together 'a few local friends interested in education to formulate plans'.

Arthur Eustace Morgan was the University College's first Principal (1926-35). In a talk on local radio in 1927, Mr Morgan noted that the College had not developed from a pre-existing institution and was 'unhampered and unguided by a past'. The College was certainly an independent foundation but the dream of university education in Hull had been cherished for some time.

Until after the war the University College consisted of only two buildings. One contained Arts and Administration; the other, Science, the Library, and Common Rooms. In the austere post-war period the University College expanded into temporary huts, and these remained in use

until the building of the second stage of the Library in the late 1960s. The war, directly and indirectly, produced many changes. These included widespread links with colleges and schools and a greater demand for university education; but the granting of the University's Royal Charter in 1954 inaugurated a more notable period of expansion.

Lord Middleton succeeded T. R. Ferens as President of the University College, then served as the first Chancellor of the University, from 1954-1969 and thus conferred the first University of Hull degrees (rather than those of London University). The Vice-Chancellor for the first two years was Dr John Henry Nicholson who had

Above: Part of the original Library.
Top: The entire academic staff of 1929.
Left: The Founder of the University College, The Right Hon. Thomas Robinson Ferens.

been Principal of the University College from 1935. In 1964 he was succeeded by Sir Brynmor Jones, previously the G. F. Grant Professor of Chemistry, under whose guidance an award-winning complex of six halls of residence, The Lawns, was built in Cottingham, a few miles from the University, as part of a building boom which also included three major science buildings on campus; Physics, Biology and Chemistry.
By the seventies the University, under the general guidance of its consultant architect, Sir Leslie Martin, had intensively developed its site with the Middleton Hall between the two original buildings and, at the centre of an integrated campus, the square-towered Brynmor Jones Library.

In 1970 Lord Cohen of Birkenhead succeeded Lord Middleton as Chancellor, and served in that office until 1977. Professor S. R. Dennison became

Top: The Duke of York (later George VI) laid the foundation stone of the University College on 28th April 1928. Below: Post-war temporary huts being demolished in 1957 to make way for the new Library. Left: The two original buildings of the University College; Arts and Administration (left) and Science, the Library and Common Rooms (right).

After the Robbins-Report inspired boom of the sixties, for the University of Hull, no less than Britain's other established 'civic' universities, the seventies and early eighties saw a pause in the hectic pace of building, followed by the first of the many cuts in Government funding which had to be managed by the next two Vice Chancellors, Sir Roy Marshall and Sir William Taylor. Economies were succeeded by painful retrenchment, then, from the middle eighties, staff who resigned or retired were replaced only if that was necessary to the survival of teaching and research in their specialisms.

But the University proved no less resilient than the City whose name it is proud to carry. Its student numbers rose from 5,500 to nearly 14,000 in the decade from 1987 to 1997, its distance-taught programmes were carried worldwide, while each year students came to study in Hull from over 100 overseas countries, attracted both by the University's record for excellence in teaching (matched by only eight other UK universities) and by its reputation for leading-edge research in areas from computer-aided language learning to lasers, robotics, and liquid crystals. Towards the end of the same decade, in 1996, Humberside College of Health's 120 staff and 1,600 students joined the University and its Postgraduate Medical School (the latter

his Vice-Chancellor in 1972, shortly before Lord Wilberforce commenced his remarkable sixteen years service as Chancellor, from 1978 to 1994.

Top: 21 students of Aeronautics, between 1934 and 1946, returned to graduate in 1995 after their original Diploma was re-assessed as of degree status.
Above: Rag Day in 1959.
Right: The visit of the Queen in 1955. She is seen with the Chancellor, Lord Middleton and Vice Chancellor Dr. Brynmor Jones.

he helped create. It was, however, entirely appropriate that in February of 1997 - the same year in which the City and its University joined in celebrating the 150th anniversary of Ferens' birth - the current Chancellor and Vice Chancellor, Lord Armstrong of Ilminster and Professor David Dilks, attended a reception at Buckingham Palace to receive The

based at Hull Royal Infirmary but with important units in the region's other hospitals) to form a Faculty of Health. This merger represented the largest single incremental addition in the University's history: it also made Hull a two-site institution, with a second, East Riding Campus, at Willerby.

Even the visionary 'Tommy' Ferens could not have conceived such a future for the institution

Queen's Anniversary Prize for Further and Higher Education from the hands of the same monarch who, in 1955, had visited the University shortly after she had granted its charter.

Top: The Lawns, six halls of residence built in a parkland setting close to the centre of Cottingham.
Below: The 1970s campus: the two original buildings can be seen facing Cottingham road, on the left.

A full circle of service

East Yorkshire Motor Services Ltd was registered in October 1926 by the British Automobile Traction Co Ltd to take over Lee & Beulah Ltd and Hull & District Motor Services Ltd. Starting with a fleet of some 34 buses, the new company adopted Lee & Beulah's colours of dark blue and primrose.

By the end of the month four more operators had been taken over, one of them David William Burn who had moved to Hull and started a cycle building and repair shop which he ran in West Parade in the 20s. East Yorkshire had begun to establish itself as a major operator in the Hull area. Before the year ended the company took delivery of its first brand new buses, five 31-seater Leylands.

A property at Anlaby Common was acquired for offices and soon services had been established to York. By 1927 larger offices were needed and accommodation was rented in Leyton Chambers in Paragon Street.

These offices remained in use until May 1941 when when they were badly damaged in one of the many bomb attacks made on Hull. Also in 1927 Lister Street Garage was purchased for £4,500 to house the company's 30+ buses.
By now it was operating 16 routes, most of which radiated from Hull. Eleven more new Leyland buses were ordered and more local operators were taken over.

In May 1929 a new express service from Hull to Blackpool was started, together with a service to Birmingham.

These services were maintained by new Leyland 'Tiger' coaches which operated from the new depot at Anlaby Road. These premises, expanded by acquisition of adjoining property over the years, remain in use today as the company's head office and main garage.

According to figures published in 1933, East Yorkshire were then operating 145 buses and coaches over 36 routes. The next year 34 new buses and coaches joined the fleet, some with the top deck tapered inwards to allow for the Gothic arch of Beverley Bar, under which many vehicles had to pass on their way to the city centre. This remained a unique feature of almost all EYMS double-deck buses bought until 1971, when the Bar was by-passed.

In May 1936 the first strike took place. It was soon resolved and the EYMS staff returned to work. Disaster struck in 1941 when enemy action destroyed Leyton Chambers, together with most of the company records.

Surprisingly, few of East Yorkshire's vehicles were damaged, perhaps because of a scheme to park them on the street away from the garage, where they were watched over by the Home Guard.
During 1950 East Yorkshire experimented with changes of livery but public opinion sent them back to blue and primrose. However, in 1972, by then a subsidiary of the National Bus Company, EYMS had to abide by the corporate colour scheme and the buses became blue and white. Then, in 1973, further orders from on high changed them to poppy red and white.

In May 1981 the co-ordination scheme between the company and Hull Corporation, dating from 1934, was superceded by a new operating agreement. Now both operators were allowed to keep the monies earned by their buses rather than pooling these and then sharing by a pre-determined ratio.

When the new Humber Bridge opened in June 1981, East Yorkshire began a new limited-stop service from Hull to Scunthorpe, jointly with Lincolnshire Road Car Company.

With deregulation of local bus services in October 1986 the company gained a substantial number of additional contracts in the Hull area. This led to the acquisition of Cherry Coaches of Anlaby, whilst increasing competition in Hull led to the purchase of more local operators, including Metro and Rhodes, in the next few years.

1988 brought a new minibus service from Beverley to Hull, serving Hull Pier and the city's marina. It also brought a 2-week strike during the annual wage negotiations! However, this was the first significant industrial action for a very long time and generally the company has enjoyed a history of good industrial relations.

EYMS entered the 90s with the Group fleet at over 330 vehicles and a turnover of over £13 million. Since its foundation it has passed from private enterprise to being a member of a large group, then through state ownership in 1969 back to the private sector in 1987, thus completing a full circle.

Looking to the future EYMS intends to diversify whilst firmly maintaining its core business, now worth £22 million a year well into the next century.

Above: This is one of East Yorkshire's many Leyland Tiger coaches which was used on a network of express routes - known as Yorkshire Services. This one was on its way to Barnsley and Birmingham and dates from 1934.
Facing page, top: This photograph shows one of the original Lee & Beulah buses which ran the service from Brough and South Cave to Hull. The date is not known but it must have been about the time Lee & Beulah was taken over to form one of the original parts of EYMS.
Facing page, centre: This is the cover of a 1962 holiday tour brochure promoting the 'Star Tours' which were a well-known feature of East Yorkshire's coaching operations in the 1950s and 60s.
Facing page, bottom: The four coaches pictured here show the transition from the earlier half-cab type of coach to the more modern 'full-fronted' variety. The coaches date from the early 1950s and are pictured outside the main garage at Anlaby Road.
Left: This 1955 Leyland double-deck bus shows the unique roof profiling on most East Yorkshire buses until 1971.

The Thompson Group - almost a century of service to the motor industry

At the turn of the century the footsore public of Britain were slowly turning to more up-to-date methods of getting about and began buying Penny-farthing cycles.

In 1905 Mr William Leon Thompson, who had previously been employed as a cabinet maker, decided to get in on the act. He founded a pedal cycle business in Hull and ever since then the name of Thompson has been associated with Yorkshire transport.

His assistant was his wife and his premises were in Anlaby Road in Hull. At that time the British motor industry, later destined to lead the world with new ideas and developments, was unheard

Above: A fleet order of Vauxhall Cresta saloons and Bedford vans being delivered to Hawker Siddeley at Brough, home of the Blackburn Beverley air freighter.
Below: Harry Naylor, then General Manager handing over a Vauxhall Velux to another famous son of Hull, David Whitfield.

of but gradually the emphasis of his business changed from penny-farthing to pneumatic-tyred cycles to motor cycles and then to cars and trucks.

Until the thirties, Thompsons acted for the Ford Motor Company, selling, among other models, the famous Model T, the cheapest family car of its kind and the first mass-produced family car on the market.

In 1933 Thompson of Hull Ltd were appointed main Vauxhall and Bedford dealers in the East Riding and, after that date, greatly expanded the business, opening up new depots and acquiring new businesses in Scarborough and Driffield.

Building expansion progressed in step with business success. The growth of the Thompson Group was largely based on developing the service side of the motor industry in accordance with the policy of the founder and his three sons. One of these was Wing Commander J Herbert Thompson, DFC, AFC, who was captain of the Lockheed Hudson bomber which, during World War Two, captured intact the only German U-boat to be taken prisoner from the air. Before the war he had been in

Above and Left: Special commercial vehicle bodies for specialist local users built on Bedford Chassis were a common site locally.

Before the war he won many major awards at Brooklands and at speed events at Southport and Skegness. He also competed in the Ulster TT. He was a chairman of the Yorkshire Centre of the Motor and Cycle Trades Benevolent Fund. With his association with high performance cars, Bill Thompson managed the Jaguar/Daimler franchise the Group held in East Yorkshire.

> ## "IN THE 1960s, ANOTHER GENERATION OF THOMPSONS ENTERED THE BUSINESS"

In 1956 the Thompson Group acquired the large Doncaster motor firm of Ralph Edwards & Son Ltd for £50,000. Ralph Edwards had bought it for £3,750 in 1939 and disposed of it so that he could concentrate on agricultural tractors. The business continued to operate as the main Vauxhall and Bedford dealers for the Doncaster area and under Thompson direction the service side of the Doncaster business was further developed. By this time, Thompsons also had become the main Vauxhall and Bedford dealers in the East Riding with premises in Scarborough, Driffield and Goole as well as the main Hull site.

One of the companies in the group, known simply as Thompson of Hull still had its

charge of one of the firm's branch shops and afterwards he looked after the Vauxhall-Bedford side of the Thompson Group.

Another son, Lieutenant Colonel George Thompson was a former Commanding Officer of the RASC territorial unit in Hull. After the war he became managing director of the Group's Standard Triumph Dealership and also controlled a Massey Ferguson farm machinery division. The third son, W L (Bill) Thompson, was well known among car racing enthusiasts.

Above: Eric Hutchinson and Richard Thompson receiving an award for outstanding aftersales performance from Vauxhall Director, Hank Clark. Right: A picture from the sixties of new Vauxhall cars on display outside the Anlaby Road showrooms.

moved to its new purpose built premises on Clive Sullivan Way. The site of almost four acres includes enhanced showrooms, workshop and parts facilities and features an accident repair centre with the very latest hi-tech paint spraying equipment. The move is seen as essential and one which will enable the company to keep up to date with developments in modern technology while retaining the qualities of reliability and integrity on

headquarters in Anlaby Road, now a large and impressive building with almost 150 members of staff. They took pride in quality of the after sales servicing of all vehicles whether they were private cars or large trucks and their service work was especially valued by the small commercial operator who could take his vehicle into the garage after work and collect it, serviced or repaired, the following morning.

In the sixties, another generation of Thompsons entered the story. Mr Herbert Thompson's two sons, Christopher and Richard and Mr W L Thompson's son David entered the firm after various courses of study followed by National Service. This decade saw the Group expand into North Lincolnshire, and the premises at 230-236 Anlaby Road became the Company's Headquarters.

With the passage of time, Anlaby Road ceased to be the main entry into Hull and Thompson of Hull's Vauxhall garage, built in 1932, could not be adapted to meet 21st Century standards. The site was sold to the Royal Infirmary and in 1993 the company

which it has built its outstanding reputation over the last century.

Above: An impressive aerial view showing the extent of the new premises on Clive Sullivan Way.
Below: Richard and Christopher Thompson, left and centre, with Trevor Barnes, General Manager, right, outside the new premises on opening day.

Looking after the health and welfare of the community

The 'blitz' on Hull during the Second World War destroyed records which makes it difficult to trace the origin of The Health Scheme. However, there is a mention of contributions, made in 1861 and called "donations from operatives" in a history of Hull Royal Infirmary.

The existence of a 'Hospital Sunday Fund' suggests that subscriptions from workers, which covered themselves but not their families, were collected on Sundays.

There are records which leave no doubt that the Hull Voluntary Hospitals Council was formed in 1929 by the Working Men's Committee.

The HVHC's object was to raise funds in support of the hospitals of the day. Later the HVHC Contributory Scheme was formed to continue the work of the original Scheme and also to provide free treatment for contributing members and dependants in participating hospitals. The contributions at that time were 1d, 2d and 3d to cover children, pensioners and families. Amongst the benefits offered to those who paid the 3d rate were two weeks at selected convalescent homes, a home help, free physiotherapy or £1 towards a full denture. Benefits were paid after 13 weeks of membership for illnesses occurring after the expiration of this period. The staff consisted of an Organising Secretary and one assistant. The office in use in May 1941 was destroyed by enemy action so that accommodation for the staff had to be provided at the Royal Infirmary until the Health Service changes in 1948. Minutes of the meetings held to wind up the Council in 1948 and transfer the assets to the new Scheme make interesting reading. Included in the list of assets was an outstanding claim on the Board of Trade "for office furniture and fittings valued at £260 destroyed by enemy action".

The new National Health Service took over all the Voluntary Hospitals Council's funds. Countrywide, many similar schemes closed down, since all medical services were to be 'free'. However, in Hull the Council was reformed in an effort to cover those areas where the National Health Service did not operate. Even though they had no money in the bank, Council members were confident that their newly formed Scheme would prosper. They accumulated funds from contributors at the same rate and paid cash benefits to hospital in-patients and gave assistance in various other fields. The title was changed to include 'York and East Riding.'

Mr W G Nevin was secretary of the Voluntary Hospitals Council for a number of years. He was the first Honorary Treasurer of the British Hospitals Contributary Schemes Association (1948), resigning in 1956 when he was made an honorary member. A Benevolent Fund was formed in 1949. From then until 1958 charitable grants seem to have been confined to cases of hardship and distress arising from illness.

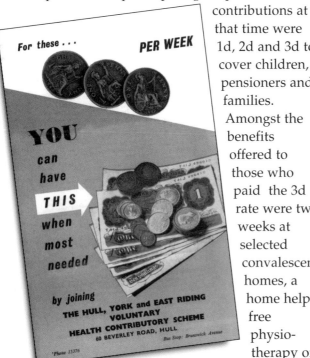

Top: Henry Chatterton, Honorary Vice President, was born in 1911 and has been a member of the Scheme since 1933. He served as director on the board from 1956 until 1994, utilising his extensive knowledge of personnel matters from his business life.
Left: An early leaflet promoting the Scheme.

From 1958 the scope was widened to include grants to hospitals, medically related organisations and charities.

In May 1955, with the Scheme re-established, offices at 60 Beverley Road were purchased and this remained the Scheme's home until in 1990 when it moved to its present address in Freetown Way.

When decimal currency was introduced in 1971, contributions were increased to a more realistic 3p a week to enable benefits to be doubled. In 1972, in anticipation of the changes in local government boundaries, there was yet another name change to the Humberside Contributory Health Scheme.

In January 1975 the standard contribution rate was increased to 6p a week and benefits were doubled as from the same date. From July 1977 the standard contribution rate was increased to 10p with an optional 3p rate for retired pensioners.

Increased benefits were also payable from this date, together with a new Private Specialist Consultation Grant.

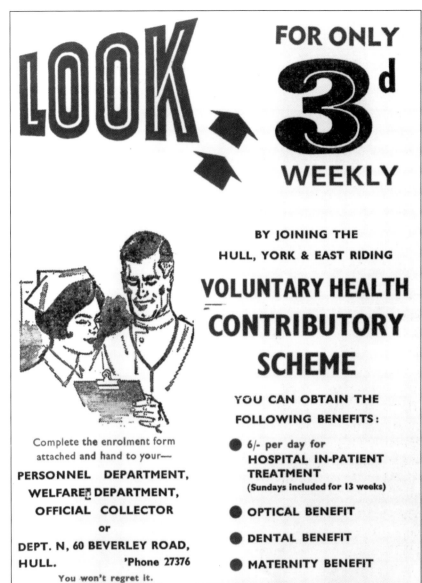

LOOK FOR ONLY **3d** WEEKLY

BY JOINING THE
HULL, YORK & EAST RIDING

VOLUNTARY HEALTH CONTRIBUTORY SCHEME

YOU CAN OBTAIN THE FOLLOWING BENEFITS:

● 6/- per day for HOSPITAL IN-PATIENT TREATMENT
(Sundays included for 13 weeks)

● OPTICAL BENEFIT

● DENTAL BENEFIT

● MATERNITY BENEFIT

Complete the enrolment form attached and hand to your—

PERSONNEL DEPARTMENT,
WELFARE DEPARTMENT,
OFFICIAL COLLECTOR
or
DEPT. N, 60 BEVERLEY ROAD, HULL.   'Phone 27376
You won't regret it.

Inflation has had its effect on the Scheme and to counteract some of the problems there were two more major changes. In April 1980 the 10p scheme was withdrawn and replaced with a 15p scheme paying

Above: A leaflet advertising benefits offered by the Hull, York & East Riding Voluntary Health Contributory Scheme from the early sixties.
Left: Ian J. Blakey, Director presenting a cheque for £10,000 to Lord Halifax at Garrowby in 1992.

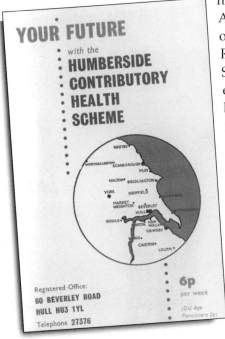

higher benefits. Also, a new optional Multi-Rate Benefit Scheme paid even higher benefit scales in return for higher contribution rates. Members could then tailor their contribution rates and benefits to suit their financial circumstances.

Trade, brought with them a wide variety of experience and expertise. Rapid growth in membership numbers brought increased income that provided for a greater value in and a wider range of benefits.

In 1992 the Scheme changed to a nationwide basis of operation. This move demanded a more appropriate and less parochial title. The all-embracing title, 'The Health Scheme' was chosen. Funded by The Health Scheme, The Health Scheme Charitable Trust is now a registered charity. Its aim is to contribute to the health and welfare of the community in areas where membership is drawn. It makes donations to NHS Trusts and to medically related projects and causes. The Trust also provides assistance to members and their families who suffer hardship arising from illness.

The late 80s saw a dramatic change in the management and fortunes of the Scheme. The impetus was provided by Keith Gorton, then Head of Marketing at Humberside College and now the Scheme's Chairman. A new generation of Directors, many with a common link to the Chamber of

*Left: A leaflet advertising the Scheme in the early seventies. **Below:** Health Scheme Chairman, Keith Gorton (second right) presenting a donation to the OSPREY "95 in 95" Spine Scanner Appeal.*

Morco Products - two centuries of success

In 1782 Thomas Bethel Morley, born in Barton on Humber, crossed the estuary to set up a company in Kingston Upon Hull, aged 24. In spite of the economic and political uncertainties of the time, Thomas managed to establish a successful marine chandelry and insurance business, as well as becoming a ship broker, trading from 36 High Street. By 1812 the business had expanded from ship broking to ship owning when it acquired the 377 ton vessel "Andrew Marvel", for approximately £7,500. A sea Captain called Marshall sailed it to the whaling grounds off Greenland on many occasions until 1834. By 1842 Thomas had been joined by his son William, and around this time William Gillett, born in 1815 in Chipping Norton, Oxfordshire, married Sarah Bond of Hull, and became associated with the Morleys. Many changes took place between then and 1899 when one of William's sons, Henry Meads Gillett, in partnership

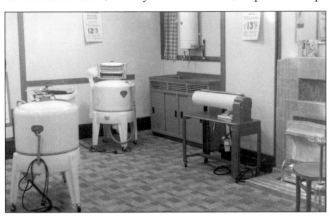

with George Jeff, formed the business into a private limited company and sold off the shipping side to a Major Clarke of Kirkella. They then opened up a lead, glass and general plumber's merchanting operation. The premises were moved from High Street to Humber Dock Side and then to Queen Street, before occupying, in 1914, a new office building and warehouses in Jameson Street and West Street. There the company remained until 1963 when it moved to it's present site in Beverley Road.

Sydney Bond Gillett, the father of the present Chairman, joined his father Henry in 1912, shortly before the First World War in which he took part, serving with great distinction as a young lieutenant in the East Riding Yeomanry. The business continued to prosper after his return from the war and an electrical wholesale department was added in 1920, followed by branch offices in Leeds, London, Newcastle and Birmingham - the London premises later becoming a casualty of the "blitz" of 1941. In 1936 an engineering factory was built in Doncaster for the manufacture of electric lighting fittings which was turned over to war work for

the Air Ministry between 1940 and 1945. After the Second World War, lighting glass imports from Continental Europe were non-existent and so Morco set up a company called Translucent Glass Limited in Wakefield to manufacture it's own glassware requirements, which still prospers today.

Richard Gillett and his brother Anthony, by now the fourth generation to work in the family firm, joined in 1949 and 1951 respectively, following their military service. Richard eventually looked after the home heating and wholesale divisions until his retirement, whilst Anthony was put in charge of the manufacturing side of the enterprise. In 1956 he became involved with caravan, leisure and marine industries and set up the L.P. Gas appliance division; initially producing a humble gas lighting fitting and later space and water heaters of all types. In 1970 a close association developed with Paloma Industries of Japan and also in 1990 with Fagor Electrodomesticos of Spain. Nowadays worldwide imports of gas appliances form the major part of the business.

Charles Gillett became the fifth generation to join the family firm (which had become Morco Products Limited in 1976) in 1987, following his University Education. It his hoped that the Gillett line will continue for many more years to come and that a company started by an 18th century entrepeneur will continue to serve its customers well into the 21st century.

Top right: The Jameson Street offices.
Left and below: Showrooms from the 40s and 50s.

Building a University out of diversity

The University of Lincolnshire and Humberside can celebrate over a hundred years of service to the local community. Higher education in Hull and the surrounding region developed rapidly after the beginning of the twentieth century, but its roots can be traced back much earlier.

It developed originally to meet a growing demand from local industry and employment as the area grew in prosperity. At the turn of the century the City Fathers determined to establish first a higher education college and later a university for the city. Capital was raised and land was bought on what was then the northern edge of the city.

In fact, several colleges were established and developed independently until they were combined into a single institution in 1976. The Hull School of Art had opened to teach applied art and industrial design in aid of local manufacturers. In 1904 it moved to Anlaby Road in Hull, premises still used by the university. In 1905, Endsleigh RC teacher training college opened and

courses in the social sciences, humanities, communications and tourism are still offered from this site.

1911 brought the Central College of Commerce providing the region's first business and commercial education. In the following year the School of Fishermen opened in Hull to provide training for the region's port and fishing industry. In 1920 it was renamed the Nautical College and moved to purpose-built accommodation in 1974. Some of the university's engineering courses can trace their origins to this college.

In 1913 Hull Training College was established on land bought by the City Fathers on Cottingham

Based in Hull, the Humberside University campus continues to strengthen its own resource base and links with local and international business. March 1998 saw the opening of the Engineering Research Centre and the relaunch of the Hull Business School. In 1997/8, students from over 50 partner institutions abroad came to study with the university. The Hull School of Art and Design won, for the second year running, the prestigious Royal Television Society National Award for Animation, the teaching staff receiving a commendation in addition to the prize won by student Ed Foster. The Hull School of Architecture's Museum & Exhibition Design Degree remains unique throughout Europe. As the university enters the new millennium it will continue to improve its high quality teaching and research.

Above: The library, 1960.
Facing page top: The Women's Common Room, 1950.
Bottom: The first male students, Cottingham Road in 1913. Below: Students study on the lawn outside the Cottingham Road Campus.

Road. The fine buildings and extensive landscaped grounds were maintained and developed over the years, providing further teaching, residential and recreational facilities for students on this campus.

In 1976 all higher education courses within the colleges were merged to form Hull College of Higher Education with one administration. Lower level courses stayed within the new college of further education in the city.

In Grimsby higher education courses in food and fisheries began in the seventies, ranging from undergraduate certificates and diplomas through to degree and post-graduate level.

In 1983 Humberside College of Further Education was created to absorb Grimsby's higher education courses, providing a wider academic environment for their further development and administration.

In 1990, the college became a polytechnic rapidly followed by conversion to university status in June 1992, allowing the institution to award its own degrees, including research (PhD) degrees.

In June 1996, the university seized the opportunity to expand further in its acquisition of a new development in Lincoln and the University of Lincolnshire and Humberside came into being. Lincoln University campus opened in September 1996 and currently stands at Phase Two, a new media centre and further student accommodation coming on line in September 1998.

Bitten by the bug to fly

Blackburn Aircraft (Blackies) holds a special place in the hearts of many Hull and East Riding families. Succeeding generations have worked there over the past eighty years through good times and not so good times. What follows is really their story...

When Robert Blackburn persuaded his father to support his attempt to design and build an aeroplane, so began events which, in a few short years would lead from canvas and string, thirty mile an hour aircraft to the high technology supersonic machines we recognise today.

Robert, or RB as he was affectionately known, graduated in engineering from Leeds University in 1907. The following year he set off on a tour of Europe to study continental engineering techniques. In France, he was fascinated to see the developments made in aviation. He returned home, bitten by the bug to fly.

Back in Leeds, with the help of a young assistant, Harry Goodyear, RB set about constructing his first aircraft. To a lesser person, the problems he encountered might well have ended the budding aviator's career before it - and he - got off the ground. But not RB. After further study and

Above: Kangaroo passenger. North Sea Aerial Navigation Co. Ltd. Leeds, Hull, London - early 1920s. *Top:* The first Blackburn design, complete with garden chair, ready for testing. *Below:* Early Mercury with RB standing on the right.

determined effort he finally achieved success on 8th March 1908 on the sands at Filey. So RB joined that select group of aviation pioneers who designed, built and flew their own aircraft.

In 1914 the 'Blackburn Aeroplane and Motor Company Limited', based at Olympia Works, Leeds, was formed, with a capital of £20,000. Government contracts which followed allowed RB the opportunity to develop his own sea planes. In 1915 a base at Brough was established and equipped. Shortly afterwards this was followed by the erection of the first hangar and

slipway to the River Humber. In 1916 the government commandeered the site and extended the facilities by building two large hangars which are still in use today.

The Kangaroo was the first pure Blackburn aircraft type to win a production contract. The end of the war marked the end of military contracts and the North Sea Aerial Navigational Company was formed using converted Kangaroo aircraft to carry passengers and freight between England and the Continent. In 1920 the Air Ministry issued a requirement for a new torpedo-

Top: Iris 111 being towed to the Brough slipway by traction engine on 25th June 1931. Below: The Roc, a fighter version of the Skua, fitted with floats and ready for trials in the Humber.
Right: Wartime maintenance on a Gipsy Moth from the Brough Flying School.

carrying aircraft and RB collaborated with Napiers, a move which was to prove a turning point in the company's fortunes. The prototype, called the Swift, was the forerunner of a range of naval bi-planes that established the Blackburn Company as specialists in the construction of naval aircraft.

In the twenties a Royal Air Force Reserve Flying Training School was set up at Brough for training both sea-plane and land-plane pilots, using Blackburn Dart, Velos, Blackburn and Ripon aircraft. This was also the era of the large flying boats, the Iris, the Sydney and the Perth, all built at Brough and making their first flights from the Humber.

With the onset of the Second World War the Blackburn Shark, a contemporary of the more famous Swordfish, was in production at Brough, along with the Skua naval dive bomber. The latter was the only British aircraft specifically built for that role. The Skua went on to be the first British aircraft to shoot down an enemy aircraft in World War Two.

With an increase in production facilities in 1939, five hundred and eighty Botha aircraft were built. The Roc naval fighter was followed by the Firebrand making its first flight in 1942. Production of it continued up to 1946. Blackburns also built 695 Fairy Barracudas at Brough, seventeen hundred Fairy Swordfish at Sherburn and 250 Sunderland flying boats at their factory in Dunbarton. In addition, Blackburns set up a modification and repair organisation for American aircraft. Between 1940 and 1945 some four thousand aircraft were dealt with. It was not uncommon at Brough to see Avengers, Wildcats and Corsairs alongside Barracudas and Firebrands on engine runs and awaiting delivery flights.

Facing page: A Beverley flying over Beverley Minster in the 1950s. **This page top:** *The Beverley sisters board a Blackburn Beverley during a visit to Brough in 1958.* **Right:** *A Blackburn Skua, the only dive-bomber produced by Britain during the Second World War.*

In 1948 Blackburns amalgamated with General Aircraft. This partnership led to the development and building of the Universal Freighter, the forerunner of the Beverley. Fifty two of these giant aircraft were built and served throughout the world supplying British forces during the fifties and sixties.

In the mid fifties the Blackburn Company renewed its association with the Navy through

Top: The Blackburn Firebrand MkIV entered service with the Fleet Air Arm just too late to see service in World War II. *Left:* Brough workers make their way to the canteen at lunchtime in April 1940.
Below: Trident fuselage production at Brough, 23rd October 1970.

the Buccaneer. The production of this plane dominated the Brough scene in the sixties. Sadly, Robert Blackburn did not live to witness the first flight of this remarkable aircraft arguably the most famous of all the Blackburn models. RB died in 1957 aged 72, having contributed forty seven distinguished years to aviation.

Although the name Blackburn disappeared from the scene in 1965, Brough has continued to play its part in the technological advances made in aircraft design and manufacture, first with Hawker Siddeley and, in more recent years, with British Aerospace.

Above: A Royal Navy Buccaneer makes a high speed low level pass over the Blackburn flight test facility at Holme-on-Spalding Moor. Below: Buccaneers under production at Brough in the 1960s.

Feeding the people for over a century

Northern Foods had its beginnings in Pape & Co Ltd, a small condensed milk importing and wholesaling business in Hull. Established originally in 1880 as a butter-importing operation in Bishop Lane, the business really began to move forward when the Horsley family took it over in the 1920s.

It was the foresight of George Horsley's son, Alec, who identified the commercial and strategic advantage of establishing a locally-based milk condensing plant, that really set the company on the road to success.

The plant was built in 1937 at Holme on Spalding Moor. From its completion Alec never looked back and five years later when he registered the business as Northern Dairies, it had grown considerably.

After the war he built up a substantial and successful dairy concern. It became a public company in 1956 and by the early sixties it stretched from Middlesbrough to Northampton and westwards to North Wales and Northern Ireland.

In 1970 Alec retired as Chairman and was succeeded by his son Nicholas. By then the profits had risen to well over £1 million. Alec remained an active member of the board till 1987 and, until his death in 1994, was Honorary President of Northern Foods. Aware of its dependence on the dairy market, the company had been diversifying for some time. With Nicholas at the helm the pace of this change of emphasis increased. In 1972 the name of the business changed to Northern Foods to reflect the widening interest in cakes, meat products, biscuits and later chilled foods.

Alec's son-in-law, Chris Haskins succeeded Nicholas in 1986 and the company continued to grow apace. The acquisition of Express Dairies and Eden Vale in 1992 made Northern the leading firm in the UK Dairy industry, a position it held on to despite the savage rationalisation of the nation's doorstep milk facilities in the mid 1990s.

Since then the priorities of the two parts of the business have required a very different focus which lead to the demerger of the Dairy Operations to form Express Dairies plc in early 1998.

Today Northern Foods is one of the UK's leading fresh food producers with over 40 plants, and around 21,500 employees. It is the foremost supplier of high quality, high added value chilled prepared foods under the own label brands of major retailers. Additionally, it has a strong branded presence in biscuits, fresh chilled dairy products, frozen food and savoury pastry products.

Above: *Delivering milk in the 1930s.*
Left: *Northern Foods head office.*

ARCO - *adapting to the tide of change*

ARCO was established in 1884 to supply a range of rubber products to industry although some manufacturing was undertaken. It is said to have included the production of tennis balls for a then little-known championship in Wimbledon. The company moved from London to Hull in 1890 because of the shipping trade. The first Thomas Martin became Managing Director in 1907 and after a distinguished career in the Navy his son, the second Thomas Martin, succeeded his father. He bought out the majority of outside shareholders to make ARCO a truly family concern.

Things did not always go smoothly. In May 1941 an enemy bomb destroyed all of the company's sales records. It could have signalled the end but not one customer failed to settle all accounts.

From its base in Kingston upon Hull the company has grown from a small jobbing merchant into the country's leading supplier of personal protective equipment, workwear and engineering consumable products, operating from a network of twenty-one branches across the UK.

In 1960 ARCO moved to new purpose-built premises in Waverley Street, Hull. The third Thomas Martin had joined the firm in 1959 and his brother Stephen in 1964.
Together they embarked on a vigorous expansion programme, establishing branches throughout the country by acquisition and by development on green field sites.

The eighties saw a huge flourish of expansion, followed by a period of consolidation in the early nineties, though even then growth did not stop.

Throughout its history the company and the Martin family who own and manage the business have been enthusiastic in their support of the Hull community. The present Tom Martin attributes ARCO's success to "determination and the ability to adapt to changing circumstances...... We are looking forward to carrying the best of our traditional values into the 21st century."

Above: *A turn of the century picture of ARCO's shop in Hull.*
Left: *One of a range of leaflets from the 1960s giving information on some of ARCO's products.*
Right: *Some of the workwear produced by ARCO in the 1960s.*

One hundred not out for Oswald T. Hall

The ability to respond positively to change over the course of many decades is not normally the kind of attribute you would associate with a family firm. Those family firms that do survive for three generations or more tend to be the exception rather than the rule in the vast majority of cases, particularly in these highly competitive times.

Yet Hull based Oswald T. Hall Limited is a Company that has done just that. As one of the area's leading wholesale fresh meat and frozen food suppliers,

Top: The founder Oswald Tyerman Hall.
Below: The shop on Holderness Road in the 1920s.

Oswald T. Hall Ltd has gained a reputation for quality and service envied by its competitors. The company has an ability to respond positively and innovatively in a market that has seen many changes and a considerable amount of upheaval over the last one hundred years.

The strong position currently enjoyed by the grandsons of the founder has been built on the groundwork of the founding father of the company. The company's history makes for an interesting read, demonstrating the need to react to constantly changing market conditions.

Founded in 1898 by Oswald T. Hall with a single retail butcher's shop on Holderness Road in Hull, the company's early business was concentrated on supplying quality fresh meat to the local community and expanding from the original one shop to eight and building its own abattoir in Naylor Street. The abattoir enabled the company to maintain strict quality control of fresh beef, pork and lamb carcasses it produced so that it could be sold to Smithfield Meat Markets in London and the company's own retail shops.

Sadly in 1942 the German Luftwaffe on a bombing raid to Hull missed Saltend oil refinery and hit the abattoir with their bombs, destroying the site completely. A new warehouse at 94/95 Witham, half a mile away from the original site was purchased and new cold store built. At this time the company started to sell fresh fruit and vegetables.

The fresh fruit and vegetables were purchased daily from Humber Street vegetable market.

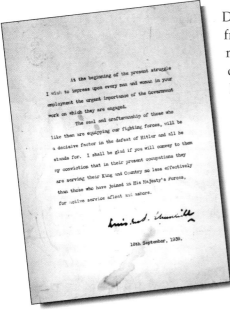

Deliveries of fresh fruit were made door to door in East Hull by horse and cart.

After the war O. T. Hall's son Terry returned to take over running the business.

For the next ten years Terry Hall expanded the business to supply shipping and trawlers arriving in Humber ports. In those days the ship's master had the total authority to purchase stores from who ever he chose. Therefore it was essential to be the first

Above A letter from Winston Churchill in 1939, reminding staff that their work was every bit as important as that of the soldiers on the front line. Below: A delivery van pictured in 1933.

person up the gangway when a vessel docked at whatever time of day to get the master to give you his order.

During the post war period of 1945/52, the British Isles had meat rationing and all families had to produce a ration card to give to their butchers. The butcher then had to sell meat at pre-set Government prices. For example; Fillet steak was 3s 4d (17p), Topside Beef was 3s (15p) and Leg of Pork retailed at 2s 10d (13p).

In 1947 Oswald T. Hall became a Limited Company. As the company expanded further contracts with major shipping companies such as Ellerman Wilson Line, Associated Humber Line, Cayzer Irvine, Bank Line, Blue Funnel Line, Nigerian National Line, Indian Steam Ship Company, Palm Line, United Baltic Corporation, Hellyers and Henriksens were negotiated. For many years whilst these shipping companies sailed the oceans of the world Oswald T. Hall Limited supplied fresh meat and vegetables and dry stores for their crews.

Sadly in May 1952 Oswald T. Hall the company founder died. Terry Hall continued to expand the business by diversifying into supplying catering

establishments with not only fresh meat but also a small selection of frozen foods that was now becoming more readily available. Terry was joined in 1966 by his son and grandson of the founder, Jeremy Hall and in 1970 Jonathan Hall, the second grandson joined the family business.

During the seventies the British Government sent frigates to Iceland to support the British trawlers and the Cod War began. However after considerable political discussion the British Government capitulated and the British trawler fleet was unable to fish within a forty-mile radius off Iceland. At the beginning of the seventies the Company were supplying between thirty and forty trawlers every month with frozen meat. With the conclusion of the Cod war,

> "WITH THE CONCLUSION OF THE COD WAR CAME THE DEATH KNELL FOR THE BRITISH FISHING INDUSTRY"

came the death knell for the British fishing industry and by the end of the decade there were no vessels sailing from Hull to the fishing grounds. Between 1976 and 1980 there was a period of consolidation due to down turn of trade.

During the early eighties due to the expansion of the high street supermarket and the prospect of out of town trading being developed the company decided to close their five retail outlets. It then developed wholesale deliveries of fresh meat and frozen foods to canteens; restaurants, shipping, public houses and the catering trade.

In 1983 Terry Hall, the son of the founder, retired although he continued to maintain an active

This picture: *Terry Hall the founder's son, pictured in 1955.*

Above: One of the retail outlets stocked for Christmas in late 1937.

interest in the business. The Witham cold store and offices proved to be inadequate and in 1986 a more appropriate site had to be found. In October of that year the Company acquired W. Duffill Frozen Food wholesalers and moved into new purpose built meat cutting plant, cold store and offices. The company could expand into frozen food distribution by adding frozen potato products, vegetables, fish, pies and pastries, ice cream and desserts to the fresh and frozen meats it already sold.

The company's manual accounting system was now replaced with modern fully integrated computerised accounting systems.

In 1991 the Company acquired Bradken Enterprises. This business specialised in supplying the fast food industry with burgers and pizza products and continental cheeses and meats. At the beginning of 1993 the company agreed to a redesign of the meat cutting plant. With consultation as to the final design from the Meat and Livestock Commission the building work began.

The existing plant was demolished and a total new factory built in its place. When the work was completed the board applied for an EEC cutting licence. This was duly approved in May of that year.

In 1996 the Company acquired Hedon Food Retail Sales Division further expanding the company's retail sales distribution and Q Food Wholesaler Meat Division further expanding the companies wholesale meat distribution.

Today's company has over twenty-five highly motivated employees, its own sales team and a refrigerated transport division delivering daily to a seventy-mile radius of Hull. The Company has succeeded in building a broad based business not only supplying fresh meat and frozen foods in Yorkshire but also exporting frozen food all over the world.

Adapting to change will remain the hallmark of this expanding and successful family business. If you are eating quality fresh meat or frozen food in Yorkshire it could well have originated from Oswald T. Hall Limited.

The Fenner Group - a long way from Twenty-one-and-a-half Bishop Lane

The Fenner Group was founded in 1861 when the young Joseph Henry Fenner set up in business in rented rooms at Twenty-One-and-a-Half, Bishop Lane, Hull.

His skills as a leather worker were channelled into the manufacture of leather belting which formed the link between the driving engines and driven machines of the day.

In 1893 the company moved to Marfleet in Hull and growth was steady throughout the succession of father to son and then to grandson.

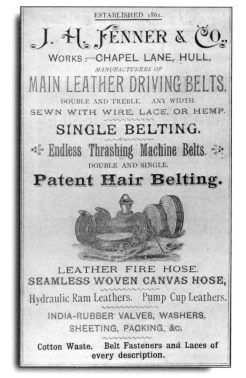

In 1921 Fenner began developing woven textile belting and was soon producing some of the finest transmission belting on the market, at the same time developing processes that would form the basis of Fenaplast Conveyor Belting some 30 years later.

With the advent of the electric motor came endless rubber V-belts from the USA. Using to full advantage the rubber technology developed in the mid 1920's the first Fenner-manufactured V-belts left the Marfleet factory in 1937 - followed by pulleys a year later.

In 1941 the main Marfleet factory was destroyed by bombing and shadow factories in Lancashire and West Yorkshire took over the company's wartime production. In addition to much-needed power transmission products, nearly 3,000,000 feet of woven canvas hose was produced for the fire fighting services.

Rebuilding commenced in Hull in 1947 and Fenner began a period of worldwide expansion - new products were introduced and companies acquired to give the Group a more diversified base from which to operate.

Today, the Fenner Group is within the top 400 UK listed companies, employs over 3900 people worldwide, with annual turnover in excess of £266,500,000 and administered from the Group Headquarters based on the outskirts of Hull. The main thrust of the Group's activities now lie in the conveyor belting and reinforced polymer fields where the Group is a dominant force in the markets in which it operates across five Continents.

The Fenner Group has come a long way from Twenty-One-and-a-Half Bishop Lane!

Top left: Joseph Henry Fenner, the founder and sole proprietor from 1861 to 1886. Centre left: The Fenner stand at the 1904 Yorkshire Show. Top right: Product range advertisement from a Hull Directory for 1877. Below: Machinery driven from overhead lineshaft by Fenner-manufactured flat leather belting.

Fenner Conveyor Belting - providing conveying solutions worldwide

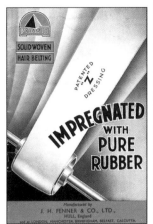

Fenner Conveyor Belting is the largest of the Fenner Group's Divisions and has been manufacturing conveyor belting for over seven decades. The Hull-based Divisional Headquarters controls the Group's conveyor belting manufacturing and marketing operations worldwide including production facilities in UK, USA, Canada, Australia, South Africa, China and India.

Fenner is the world's second largest manufacturer of heavy-duty conveyor belting and is unrivalled in its global coverage, range of products, and technical leadership in product design, manufacture and product application.

The principal products manufactured by the Division are heavy-duty solid-woven, rubber ply and steel cord conveyor belting aimed at a wide range of industrial applications including coal and hard-rock mining, aggregates, power generation, forestry, steel foundries, grain handling and bulk shipping terminals.

Following the Cresswell Colliery disaster in 1950 where 80 miners lost their lives when a rubber and canvass conveyor belt was ignited by friction, Fenner, working in close conjunction with the National Coal Board, launched a programme

of research into the production of fire-resistant conveyor belting. The result was Fenaplast, a solid-woven PVC impregnated conveyor belt first manufactured in Hull in 1952 and now used by mining and extractive industries worldwide.

Today, the Hull plant operates state-of-the-art manufacturing and testing equipment capable of

producing high tensile conveyor belts up to two metres wide. Over 190 people are employed at the Hull plant with a substantial volume of the output going to export markets - providing conveying solutions worldwide!

Top left: *Early catalogue for rubber-impregnated, solid-woven hair belting, the forerunner of Fenaplast conveyor belting.* **Centre left:** *1950 newspaper headline announcing the Creswell colliery disaster.* **Bottom left:** *The weaving department at the Marfleet site in 1930.* **Top right:** *The conveyor belting weaving department at Marfleet today.* **Above:** *Solid-woven carcass of Fenaplast conveyor belting.* **Below:** *Fenaplast conveyor belting awaiting despatch from Hull to mining operations worldwide.*

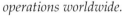

The Kings Town Group - half a century of service to the printing industry

It was in August 1946 that Eric Wright, Fred Laeser and Bertrand Best set up a company in Derringham Street, Hull, to engage in the manufacture of letterpress plates for the letterpress printer. They were well qualified to succeed as Messrs Wright and Best had previously been etchers in a firm in Leeds and Hull respectively, whilst Mr Laeser had been a printer on metal.

They stayed there two years, working to the sound of their next door neighbour's chickens and to a background of rambling roses down the yard which surprised such customers who progressed beyond the front office. The lively and

expanding business soon outgrew the limited space available there even though additional property had been taken across the road, which relieved congestion for a while but made supervision increasingly difficult.

With the move to Leads Road, Stoneferry, restricted working space with line, half tone and colour operating side by side gave way to separate departments under individual supervision. For the time, layout was spacious and well lit, permitting the introduction of much new equipment. The photo engraving department, for example, had original plate making, coupled with a first rate studio

service. Other services included a specialist art group.

The Kings Town Engraving Company Ltd was very proud of the automatic focusing on its vertical camera. Before an exposure could be taken a sheet of copper had to be coated with light-sensitive glue. In metal printing, negative and sensitised metal had to be held in perfect contact throughout exposure by a vacuum pump. Another innovation was a 'New Series' centrifugal etching bath which had replaced their old 'Mark Smith' type paddle bath.

Proofing was by 'modern' cylinder presses, reproducing as nearly as possible actual machine room conditions. Staging, the basis of all good colour work in those days, meant meticulous stopping out by the colour etcher.

Top right: Staging a half-tone plate in the tone etching department. *Left:* The camera studio in the late 1940s. *Below:* A photograph of the personnel in the early days at Stoneferry.

The in-house magazine for December 1952 shows Company Secretary Mr S Birch (in charge of accounts) sitting at a table with a pen and many sheets of paper.

1998 brings the 50th anniversary of that move to Leads Road. Although the business is still run from there the present owners, Mr Roger Parker, his wife Judith and his son William run things far differently. Gone are the whirlers (coating machines), etching baths routers, bevellers, bowlers (rotary planing machines), photographic plates on glass, acids, zinc and copper. All have been replaced by photographic film and polymer plates in the service of repro platemaking for the food packaging, pharmaceutical and toiletry industries. These are the company's main markets in the UK, whilst 2-piece can Beers/Lagers/Soft Drinks are their main customers abroad.

*Left: The company's logo. **Top left:** The etching department, showing the etching baths. **Top right:** Hand planning in the planning department. **Below:** The Lord Mayor of Hull, Councillor Harry Woodford during his Mayoral visit to Kings Town Engraving when he was presented with "The Freedom of Kings Town".*

From Canadian Prairies to the City of Hull

The personal attention to every detail and a guaranteed first class building service that has become the trademark of Robinson and Sawdon Ltd. explains the great success of the Hull-based builders over the past 76 years. The company has played a significant role in shaping North Humberside and has been responsible for creating many of the buildings which are familiar landmarks in and around Hull.

The story of Robinson and Sawdon Ltd. began in the December of 1915, on the edge of the Canadian prairies 1,000 miles west of Montreal, with a knock on the front door of Fred Robinsons home in Port Arthur. There was several feet of snow on the ground and Fred, a bricklayer from Hull who had emigrated four years earlier was surprised to hear

the stranger say "My name is Arthur Sawdon. I am a bricklayer from Hull and have just arrived in this one horse town. Can you put me up for the night until I find Lodgings?"

After ten years in Canada, Fred Robinson returned to Hull in 1921 to establish his own business. His first commission was to build a bungalow at the corner of Cottingham Road and Ferens Avenue for a Mr Lazenby, a director of Needlers, the chocolate manufacturers.

*Top right: An artists impression for the Porter Street flats. **Above:** The Robsaw Royals baseball team, Denis Robinson is standing second right. **Right:** The Half Moon at Elloughton completed in 1939.*

History repeated itself the following year when he answered a knock on the door of his home in King's Gardens to be greeted by Arthur Sawdon, "We met in the mid-west of Canada in 1915" he said "I understand that you have started on your own. Do you want a partner?"

The two men worked seven days a week, aiming to build a business with a reputation for good work, personal service, fast completion and highly competitive pricing. Their efforts paid off and by the mid twenties, Fred Robinson and Arthur Sawdon formed a limited company and began working for local authorities as well as building private dwellings. Early notable projects were three housing estates at Beverley - the Swinemoor Lane, Cherry Tree and Admiral Walker estates.

The steady growth continued into the thirties, with more housing estate contracts, industrial work and several school building programmes including Fifth Avenue School, two schools in Endyke Lane, one in Hill Road as well as the Sacred Heart Catholic School. This was followed by some church work and they also built some four and five storey blocks of flats in Porter Street.

Richard (Dick) Sawdon and Denis Robinson, sons of the founders, joined the company during the 1930s

Robinson and Sawdon Ltd. played a major role in creating a complete city from the badly bombed, rubble strewn streets of Hull.

Over the next three decades they have undertaken a wide variety of projects including, roads and sewers, industrial units, processing mills, warehouses, engineering works, fish processing factories, houses, law courts, city centre office blocks, swimming pools, gas terminal works, public houses and fifteen schools. Demonstrating the company's versatility and flexible policy of tackling any type of building work no matter how large or small.

having successfully completed building apprenticeships and becoming Fellows of the Institute of Building. With the onset of war Denis joined the armed forces and Richard worked for the Royal Engineers on coastal defence projects but sadly Arthur Sawdon died suddenly in May 1940 at the age of 50. Fred Robinson steered the company through the war years, building large air-raid shelters for industry and carrying out war damage repair work. They were also main sub-contractor to the Admiralty working round the clock replacing fire-bricks in the boilers of Royal Navy and Merchant Navy vessels.

Dick and Denis resumed working for the company after the war and gradually Fred Robinson handed over full control of the company to them.

The company, now based on English Street, has established an impressive reputation for reliability and technical expertise and for delivering the same high standard of service first set by its founders. Today their grandsons, Mike and Bob Sawdon and Charles Robinson (the third generation) are looking forward to the future with optimism and continue to maintain the same high standard of workmanship that has won the company many architectural awards over the decades. Robinson and Sawdon Ltd. look set to continue to deliver that same commitment to personal service and integrity which has always been the company's firm foundation.

Top left: The award winning Riley Technical School, built in 1957. Top right: The nearby premises of George Lodge and Sons Ltd, English Street, built in 1962. Left: A building completed in 1960, Tivoli House on Paragon Street. Below: The Waterloo Tavern built for Bass Breweries in 1987.

George Lodge & Sons Ltd

Mr George Lodge, with the money he had made from buying and selling cutlet, founded a business which he described as "Machinery and Metal Merchants" in 1880. Goods sold included Pulleys, Blacksmiths Tools, Lifting Tackle, Safes etc. Three of the founders sons Albert, Percy and Herbert worked in the business along with their father.

WROUGHT IRON PULLEYS ARE THE BEST.

WALKER STREET,
HULL, ... 191

Corp. Tel. 1431.

Memo from Geo. Lodge & Sons,
Metal & Machinery Merchants.

To M ....

WRITE FOR PRICE.

All kinds of Engineers', Boiler Makers' and Blacksmiths' Tools, Engines and Boilers, Shafting, Pedestals, Pulleys, Lathes, Drilling and Shaping Machines, Saw Tables, &c. New and Second-hand Patent Blocks, Screw Jacks, Crabs, and other Lifting Tackle, for Sale or Hire.

Dealers in Office Furniture, Shop Fittings, Safes, &c.

TERMS CASH. Goods Bought on Commission at Sales by Auction or Private Treaty. All Goods offered subject to being unsold.

In 1920
The bearing manufacturers Ransome & Marles Ltd. offered the company an agency for their products and the use of their logo, the one still used by the company today. The appointment by R & M coincided with the fourth of the founder's sons, another George, a qualified Marine Engineer joining the business. This opened up the opportunity of selling new and second hand machine tools, electric motors and developing the bearing business.

The Walker Street site was little more than a large field with stables for offices and warehouses. Despite that the Lodge family were not happy when the site was compulsorily purchased during the 1950's and the business moved to English Street. However, the opening of the Clive Sullivan Way gave easy access to Britain's motorway network and the move eventually worked very much to the company's advantage.

Today the firm distributes to many parts of the British Isles,

but the main core of the customer base is still local companies in the Shipping, Fishing, Food processing and manufacturing industries, some of whom have been loyal to the company for over 70 years.

A third George Lodge entered the business in the 1950s - a far sighted man who re-profiled the items stocked and sold in accordance with what he believed would best serve the customers in the future. Machine Tools and Electric Motors he felt were best left to companies specialising in such products. He felt his company could offer its customers a better service by stocking a comprehensive range of bearings, oil seals, Transmission Products, Belts and Lubricants.

The fourth George Lodge did not enter the business, he followed his vocation as a doctor. The firm, however, still operates as a modern family business with a dedicated staff who offer a 24 hour service every day of the year.

There are customers who still reminisce about the Walker Street site, they obviously feel it had more charm than the well organised high-tec site the company uses today.

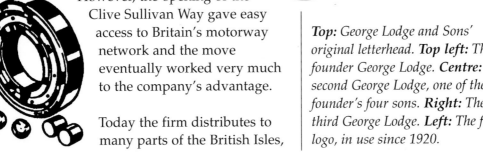

*Top: George Lodge and Sons' original letterhead. **Top left:** The founder George Lodge. **Centre:** The second George Lodge, one of the founder's four sons. **Right:** The third George Lodge. **Left:** The firm's logo, in use since 1920.*

In control of industry's power

The Humber Electrical Engineering Company was established by William Ernest Shuttleworth. He was born at Lothersdale in the West Riding and trained at Wolverhampton, arriving in Hull to work at Earles Shipyard as Electrical Manager. In 1908 he left Earles to form his own electrical company, and in 1911 moved to Portland Place where the company still has its Headquarters.

From the beginning the firm specialised in complete electrical installations on ships and was a pioneer in the fitting of electric light on trawlers. Indeed WE Shuttleworth patented and manufactured several trawler light fittings which were in use until quite recently. Small DC generating sets were also designed and manufactured, and in one year alone over fifty ships at Swansea had his sets installed. Teams of men worked at ship yards all over the country.

As a result of many enquiries, the Company undertook its first land installations in 1926, when many farms and country estates received electricity for the first time. The New Theatre in Hull was one of their prestigious jobs prior to the War. During the Second World War the Company's entire resources were geared to the war effort, including the complete electrical installation on Coastal Minesweepers, Corvettes and a large number of merchant ships. Altogether work was completed on over 160 new vessels.

After the War, Humber Electrical was closely involved in the rebuilding of many well known local landmarks, including Hammonds, Willis Ludlow, the Co-op and Drypool Bridge. Originally all electrical equipment had to be manufactured and designed in-house because it was not possible to nip down to the local wholesalers and buy equipment off the shelf as it is today. Switchboards would be manufactured with an open front and have knife switches mounted on slate or a type of fibre board. Nowadays switchboards are what is called "dead front" which means that all the electrical parts are fully insulated and shrouded from accidental damage.

Mr SN Shuttleworth, the only son of Mr WE Shuttleworth joined the company in 1933, followed by his son Mr CE Shuttleworth who joined the company in 1975 and is now Managing Director Today after investing heavily in computerised equipment, the Company is working throughout the UK, the rest of Europe, Japan and South America. They are involved in all aspects of electrical engineering for marine and off-shore industries, the MoD, public authorities and many large industries.

Top left: The founder W.E. Shuttleworth.
Above: One of the merchant ships fitted with electric light by the company.
Left: An early advertisement for the Humber Electrical Engineering Company.

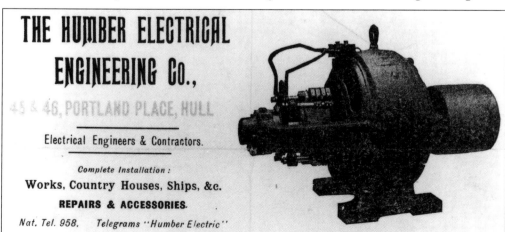

THE HUMBER ELECTRICAL ENGINEERING Co.,

45 & 46, PORTLAND PLACE, HULL

Electrical Engineers & Contractors.

Complete Installation :
Works, Country Houses, Ships, &c.
REPAIRS & ACCESSORIES.

Nat. Tel. 958.   Telegrams "Humber Electric"

C. B. North Ltd. quality and service in timber

The North family can be traced back in the Hull area to the 1740s but Charles Matthew North was the first member to be in the timber trade. Starting in 1863 as a joiner in Lee Smith Street, Hull, he later worked as a packing box maker in Prospect Place, Drypool.

C. M. North & Co was formed in 1874 as packing case makers also in Prospect Place.

Mr C. M. North's son William traded as a timber merchant, first in Lockwood Street, then in Lime Street and Sitwell Street, in the name of W. W. North. William became a councillor and alderman of the city. The family still possesses a medal he received on the opening of Pickering Park. He formed the company W. W. North Ltd in 1913.

Company accounts for 1913-14 show income and expenditure for a vessel, the SS Malta which was later renamed Ethel after one of William's daughters. It is presumed the ship was owned by William North and operated through the company to import timber. A 6ft long profile of the ship is displayed in the company offices.

Clifford North, the youngest of William's eleven children, was born in 1903 and joined the business on leaving school. When William died in 1937, Clifford North formed his own company, C.B. North Ltd with one of his brothers, Bramwell. After a short while Bramwell left to pursue other interests. Meanwhile the older brothers continued the North family's Box Mills business which operates today as NBM Timber Products Ltd.. C. B. North Ltd traded throughout the Second World War on a reduced scale whilst Mr North served in the RAF. One of his first war duties was to operate barrage balloons on barges on the River Humber to bring down enemy aircraft. However, these did not prevent most of the company's premises being badly damaged during air raids in 1941.

Clifford North was released from the RAF in 1944 to resume full time charge of the business. Bomb

Above: Staff of W W North, Sitwell Street in 1921.
Below: C B North's sheds at Victoria Dock in 1939. The driver in the vehicle on the right is T C Norman.

damage was repaired and expansion took place through the purchase of other properties in the area. Clifford's two sons, the fourth generation, joined the company, Keith in 1951 and Ian in 1959. A stockist agreement with Formica was signed in 1955 and with Cape Building Products in 1957. Their products are still stocked by the company today.

During the sixties the emphasis was on expansion and modernisation. Sheds of 75,000 square feet were built to enable loading and more storage of timber to be under cover. Side loaders replaced forklift trucks as they allowed timber to be carried the 'natural' way on the road. In 1973 a timber treatment plant was installed and in 1976 the manufacture of computer-designed timber roof trusses began.

Keith and Ian North continued the business when their father died in 1977. After finishing his university course in 1988, Richard North was the first of the fifth generation of the family to enter

the business. Brother Andrew followed him in 1992. In 1994 new offices were built so that all the business is now on one four acre site at 65 Hedon Road. In 1995, Ian North left the business to pursue other interests.

Early introduction of modern methods of production, transportation, computers and communications have always been an important factor in keeping ahead of competition, providing customers with what they want when they need it.

C.B. North Ltd. currently employ 45 staff and continue to import timber and wood based sheet materials. Customers range from the smallest cash sale to several of the country's national house-builders. Services offered to customers include design and manufacture of roof trusses, timber grading, treatment, sawing and planing, with their own fleet of transport delivering nationwide. The company looks forward to progressing well beyond the year 2000.

*Top: The premises at 72 Hedon Road pictured in 1939. **Above:** Loading roof trusses to keep apace of the demand in todays busy market. **Right:** Generations two to five. W.W. North left, C.B. North right "on the wall". Keith North seated centre with sons Andrew, left and Richard, right.*

The story of Ma Brown

Mrs Emily Brown was actually born in Scotland but when, in the twenties, she went into business with her elder son David, she already considered herself a Beverley woman.

During the Second World War Mrs Brown had a barrack gate tea and snack bar which stood just outside a side entrance to Victoria Barracks and close to a camp formerly occupied by Polish troops, where she came to be affectionately known to thousands of servicemen as "Ma Brown".

They ran a cycle shop, first set up in a backyard in Lorraine Street, Stoneferry, Hull. Then, in 1930, she and David established the Queensgate filling station near Victoria Barracks.

Within a few months they had laid the foundations of a viable transport undertaking. From two lorries, the business soon operated thirty five long distance lorries engaged in a nightly truck service to London, with a secondary service to Liverpool.

Contract services were also operated for Ford Motors to London and Dagenham.

Mrs Brown's other son George joined the business soon after it was established.

Above: Petrol pumps at the Queensgate Filling Station on Victoria Road. Top right: An Atkinson truck on one of its many trips to London. Top left: An eight wheeler Atkinson with a 6LW Gardner powered engine. David Brown is on the left of the picture.

Following the Second World War the business was nationalised but the Browns came back into the business following demobilisation. Until she was seventy six years old, Mrs Brown took an active part in running the firm, maintaining the filling station and serving the customers herself. Two years later, in October 1964, she sadly died. For years afterwards her son David received enquiries about his mother from ex-servicemen in all parts of the country.

A notable feature of the trunk vehicles in the fleet was the elaborate headboard depicting an elephant's head. Their slogan proclaimed 'Hull and London Nightly Trunk Service'. Browns relied chiefly on the slow but very dependable Gardner powered Atkinson trucks.

Today the business is run by Michael and Roy Brown and the company currently employs fifteen people. E. Brown and Son are ideally situated to service their clients in the shipping industry, mainly with Spedition Services, Marrick Marine Company and Sea Wheel.

After sixty successful years in the haulage industry Ma Brown's initial aim to provide work for herself and her family has been more than fulfilled. It seems that the family run business can look forward to even more success in the years to come.

Above: An early picture of a trunk vehicle with its elaborate headboard depicting an elephant's head. Top left: The new body building shop at Victoria Road. Right: The old body building shop bought by Browns in 1960. Below: One of todays fleet of ERF trucks.

Charting the way for mariners worldwide

Born in 1812, Barnard Cooke followed his brother Thomas in rejecting his father's occupation of shoemaking in favour of the study and making of optical instruments. Thomas became a manufacturer of telescopes and Barnard worked with him as an optician. They established their company in Hull in 1863.

By 1872 Barnard's business had moved to Savile Street. His family were opticians and sewing machine agents, an unusual combination. Later they also became chronometers and clockmakers.

Barnard died in 1887 and no records exist to tell who ran the business in the years afterwards, though it is known to have moved to Paragon Street.

House, Alfred Gelder Street. By the next year they were listed as a limited company of nautical instrument makers.

In 1933 there was a further move to Market Place at the junction with Scale Lane. This building was badly damaged during the Second World War but the company remained there for 25 years. In 1958 they moved to their present premises at 58/59 Market Place Hull also known as the Kingston Observatory. The building consists of four floors, on the ground floor is a large retail showroom with an extensive stock of binoculars, telescopes, compasses, optical instruments, watches, clocks and barometers. The company is a British Admiralty Chart agent and stocks navigational charts for marine use. The chart room is on the first floor and carries full worldwide coverage consisting of some 4000 charts. The remaining space in the building is devoted to the companies manufacturing activities, their main product is the ships magnetic compass which is supplied to new ships, building at shipyards throughout the world. The company is well renowned for the quality of its instruments which are all hand-made.

Top: Barnard Cooke in the mid 1800s.
Left: B. Cooke and Son, also known as the Kingston Observatory at the Market Place premises in the early 1930s.
Below: Cookes Cabin, their new shop in Hepworth's Arcade.

In 1918 the business was sold to the London firm Henry Hughes who sent Mr Stacey Dickinson from their branch there to manage it under their own name. By 1925 however the premises was again listed under the Cooke name. In the Directory for that year they are referred to as "opticians, nautical instrument and compass makers and adjusters and wireless dealers."

Soon afterwards Mr Dickinson bought the business from Hughes's, poached their apprentice Ben Saferty and moved the business to Monument

Carving a niche in the British engineering industry

JF Appelbe & Company was established in Hull as the result of the toss of a coin. The engineering company had as its original partners a Mr Dunn of Sunderland and Jack Fuller Appelbe of Hull. The business having been settled in this way, the two ex-seamen-engineers set up their company in 1919.

They began as ship repairers and general engineers, working locally and for long hours to meet the demanding timetables of ships' sailings. They prospered and, by 1931, had moved to Salthouse Lane, taking additional premises in Great Union Street. They operated from the two sites until 1937 and then remained at Great Union Street until a final move in 1971 to their present home, a purpose-built factory at Littlefair Road, Hedon Road, Hull.

> "THE COMPANY WAS ESTABLISHED IN HULL AS THE RESULT OF THE TOSS OF A COIN"

During the Second World War the company undertook a lot of work for the armed forces, especially with marine support equipment, and maintaining the barrage balloon barges on the River Humber.

Mr Dunn had left the business in 1931 and later Mr Appelbe's two sons, Alec and John had joined him. The company turned to installation work and machinery movement for many of the local manufacturers. Some of this work took them further afield than Hull and their reputation began to spread.

The company helped to introduce electric arc welding to the area and the supply of new welded steel components became a large part of the business. Priestman Brothers Ltd., a local excavator, crane and grab manufacturer, were a major customer during the fifties and sixties.

After Jack's death in 1961 the business flourished and outgrew its premises and in 1970 Alec and John felt brave enough to build the new factory near King George Dock. It succeeded to the extent that extensions were needed in both 1974 and 1975, almost trebling the original size. The recession of the early eighties brought short time working, soon after John's son Tony had joined the firm. The business recovered and Tony's sister Susan joined him in the business in 1982.

The business has continued to grow and develop into new markets, with a customer base now well spread over several countries in a number of markets, such as off-shore, sub-sea and original equipment makers, all of whom are supplied with high quality welded steel fabrications to their specific requirements.

Left A trawl board as manufactured until 1960.
Below: A 5 metre diameter winch drum, able to hold 4km of sub-sea umbilical cable. This would be used on seismic research vessels, converted from the fishing vessels of the old East Coast fleets.

F.R. Scott Ltd - Firm with a future

F.R. Scott Ltd was founded by the late Fred R. Scott in 1943. Fifty five years on, this family firm continues to flourish.

Fred began his working life as an apprentice for his uncle Fred Searby, Ironmonger of Great Union Street, Hull and joined the firm of F. & T. Ross Ltd in Myton Street where he worked his way up to become General Manager and Director. He continued to manage the ironmongery side of the business until 1942, when the premises were demolished and the entire stock lost during the blitz.

Nothing was left but an unquenchable spirit. Fred Scott immediately set about the salvage of the business and formed F.R. Scott Ltd on Castle Street, which included F. & T. Ross Ltd and Fred Searby, Ironmonger, and numbered some of his staff as shareholders. The company was incorporated on October 13th, 1945.

The company has changed greatly over the years to meet its customers needs. The days are gone when horse shoes, oil lamps and cast iron cooking pots were supplied from stock; now F.R. Scott Ltd carries probably the most extensive range of bolts and nuts in Humberside, together with a vast range of ironmongery and tools. Allied to this Scott's heating department will plan and execute all types of industrial heating and pipework installations. The heating department will also undertake routine maintenance of industrial and commercial systems; a twenty four hour call out service being available if problems arise.

Sadly, in September 1965 Fred Scott died at the age of 75. He was a Freeman of the City of London and was sorely missed in local circles. His son Peter, who had worked with his father for twenty years

Top left: The founder F. R. Scott.
Above: The shop on Paragon Square during the early 1960s. *Below:* A smart turn-out of staff eagerly await a works outing, circa 1945.

succeeded him as Managing Director and continued to consolidate the expansion of the business.

In the late seventies it became apparent to Peter that more space was required to cope with customer

demand, and in 1982 new premises were acquired in Canning Street, Hull - 30,000 square feet of warehouse and offices spread over three floors. There is also the added bonus of customer parking for over fifty cars.

The range of stock is so diverse that a customer was once heard to say "If Scotts haven't it - you don't need it".

The secret of Scott's continuing success is that customers' needs are of paramount importance; the service given by the counter staff, sales office and skilled heating engineers all help to make this possible. Nothing is too much trouble, no sale too small and the fleet of vans delivering throughout the county and beyond ensure that the customers' requirements are met promptly.

None of this would be possible without the dedication and

experience of its forty staff, some of whom have been at Scotts for over 40 years.

In 1981, Peter's son Robert, grandson of the founder, joined the company, so continuing the family interest within the business, and today he is Managing Director, and Peter is Chairman.

Scotts is a business based on more than fifty years experience; with its large premises, dedicated staff, caring management and renowned customer service, F.R. Scott Ltd is certainly a firm with a future.

Top: F. R. Scott Ltd's premises on Castle Street, occupied since 1943. ***Above left:*** *The premises on Portland Place pictured in 1979.* ***Below:*** *The spacious building now the home to F.R. Scott Ltd, on Canning Street.*

The setting for a snack

There are some companies in Hull whose growth reflects the development of the city itself over the course of the 20th century. One such company is Skeltons, a name long associated with quality food and friendly service.

The Skelton story began in 1931 when Arthur Skelton gave up his post as manager of a local bakery and set up a business of his own at the rear of 1, Nornabell Street off Holderness Road. At the front of the premises was a small shop and it was over the counter of this modest establishment that the first items to emerge from Skeltons' ovens were sold to the public.

Arthur's son, Harold, had followed the trade of his father and, by the age of 21, was a qualified and experienced baker. Together, father and son daily produced bread and pastries of a quality that quickly found a ready market.

The new venture succeeded from the outset and soon the first branch shop was opened on Beverley Road. Other shops followed and it became increasingly apparent that the Nornabell Street Bakery was too small to keep them all supplied. Premises were obtained in New Bridge Road which were altered and equipped so that a new bakery was soon in full production. Since it made the Nornabell Street Bakery redundant, the original bakery was closed down.

In 1938, Arthur Skelton left the area to open up two shops in Scarborough. His son Harold ran the Hull business single-handed even though it now comprised 11 retail shops. When his father died in 1957, Harold Skelton sold off the two Scarborough shops.

In 1960 Harold's son Malcolm, a qualified Chartered accountant, joined the family business. Meantime, more shops had been bought and the bakery supplying them was once more too small to cope. Freehold premises in Lorraine Street were bought. It had previously belonged to a cast stone company, and though some

Top left: The founder A C Skelton, in 1933. ***Top right:*** *Ron Skelton on the first branch delivery vehicle.* ***Left:*** *The first ever Skeltons, on Nornabell Street.*

existing structures could be used, 90% of Skeltons' requirements had to be built from scratch.

Production continued at the New Bridge Road Bakery, though the initiation of day and night shifts was still not enough to make the output sufficient for the growing number of retail outlets. Therefore, as soon as each section of the new site was finished it was put immediately into production. Within six months the new bakery was complete. Business was transferred there and the New Bridge Road premises were closed down.

At Lorraine Street the company had plenty of room in which to expand. A new butchery department was urgently needed and in 1972 work was started on this. Trade continued to flourish with the opening of new and bigger shops which saw more emphasis being put on the cooked meats side of the business.

A natural progression for the company was to open a cafe/shop and so, in 1973, the first cafe was opened in Cottingham. It proved to be very successful and there are now eight 'Quick Bite' and 'Cornerhouse' Cafes.

Today, the output of the Lorraine Street Bakery is supplemented by that of a smaller bakery in Grimsby and a fleet of some twenty vehicles ensures that the products are brought to the customer as swiftly as possible - a far cry from the thirties when

deliveries around Hull came via a box-fronted bicycle, its rider resplendent in white shirt and black bow tie.

The branch at the junction of South Street and Paragon Street has particularly strong links with Hull's history. It is located on the site of the old Tivoli Theatre where, in 1954, Arthur Lucan, better known as 'Old Mother Riley', gave his final performance before collapsing and dying in the wings.

Philip and Richard Skelton, Malcolm's sons and the fourth generation of the family, joined the business in 1985. Both are now production directors, Richard in bakery production and Philip in butchery production. Much has changed since the firm was set up but the elements on which the bakery's success was built are still in place and the friendly service is appreciated at a time when shopping is becoming increasingly impersonal.

Left: Skelton's first branch shop at 404 Beverley Road. Standing in front of the shop are left, Harold Skelton's wife Irene and right, his sister Rene Skelton.
Below: The elegant Skelton store on Newland Avenue.

A half century of progress for Hull's Cocoa pioneers

The people around Cleveland Street must have welcomed the pleasant smell of cocoa when British Cocoa Mills took over the premises at No. 145 in the late 1930s. For Kelly's Directory for 1937 shows they were *previously* occupied by Alfred Scott and Jacksons Ltd, fish manure manufacturers.

The cocoa company was formed at Tower Street, Hull in 1935 as a partnership between two Dutch entrepreneurs with connections in the cocoa industry, Meindert Kamphuys (senior partner) and Theodore Sloot. It became a limited company in 1941, having settled on Hull because of the convenience of the port for importing raw materials as well as its proximity to Holland, their home country. The original location of the business was Tower Street.

During the war a trading relationship was established with Gill & Duffus a London commodity dealer. At around this time the organisation merged with two other southern-based cocoa mills and

Top right: An early cocoa butter tanker.
Below: Looking down the River Hull to the Spillers factory in the mid 1950s.

between them became the major suppliers of cocoa products to the U.K's chocolate manufacturers. By 1947 the company had built its first overseas mill in the West African town of Takoardi, Ghana, the first origin cocoa processing factory. Tragedy was to strike the firm in the same year when one of the founders of the firm, Mr Kamphuys, was killed when his plane crashed in the Pyrenees when he was returning from a trip to Ghana. In 1951 Mr Kamphuy's widow had sold her interest in the company to Gill & Duffus. The original Tower Street premises were destroyed by fire in 1948 and so the full cocoa processing operation was transferred to the Cleveland Street site which BCM had purchased in 1941. Recently they were excavated and found to be on the site of an edible oil mill. In the mid 1950s the Tower Street factory was rebuilt in order to process Brazil nut kernels, a role it fulfiled for around 30 years until it finally closed in 1984.

senior employees' houses. Also, millers D Hurtley & Sons Ltd had premises there. Up to the 1940s BOCM stabled horses at Glass House Row.

The name of the company changed to British Cocoa Mills (Hull) Ltd., in 1957.

In the early seventies the Co-op Wholesale Flour Mill in Glass House Row ceased operating. BCM bought it, knocked down the mill and added the site

to its own so that warehouse and factory could both be in this area. Members of staff interested in the history of the site made investigations through the Local History Unit at Hull College.

They discovered that the houses there had been occupied in 1937 by a Horace Hall, engineer, Horace White, a stable foreman, Charles Ernest Nicholls, a labourer and Albert Edward Harness, foreman, all with the Co-operative Wholesale Society Ltd millers. Before that, in 1916, the street was occupied by J & J Stephenson, seed crushers, and the Bon Accord Mill of British Oil and Cake Mills Ltd., together with some of their

Top left: A 1950s view from across the river.
Top right: Carver presses (circa 1950). *Above:* The Cocoa Bean Warehouse during the 1950s.
Right: The Expeller Plant (circa 1950).

The street's name comes from a row of employees' cottages on the perimeter of the site of the Hull Glass Company. This business manufactured glass here on a site adjacent to Earle's Cement Works in the second half of the last century.

In 1988 BCM acquired office buildings to the north of Glass House Row which had also belonged to the Co-op. The buildings there were demolished by BCM and the site, together with some derelict land nearby provided room for a new Finished Goods warehouse.

In 1991 the former Slingsby's premises to the south of the site were bought and mostly demolished. Slingsbys were a firm of steel fittings stock holders who had come to the site in the 1940s.

In 1990 the company was acquired by the E D & F Man Group changing its name in 1995 to reflect its

sterilised and whole-bean roasted before cracking and winnowing to remove the lighter outer shell. The roasted nib, the valuable part of the bean, is triple-ground to produce liquor retaining the excellent flavour characteristics demanded by the chocolate industry. Alternatively, the unroasted bean is cracked and winnowed to produce raw nib. This is steamed, alkali-treated, roasted and triple-ground to produce a very fine liquor which is heated to 100 degrees centigrade. Cocoa butter is separated from cocoa solids by hydraulic pressing. The quantity of cocoa butter expressed is controlled to give the right amount of fat. The presscake is then milled into cocoa powder. Meanwhile the cocoa butter is filtered to a high degree of clarity. There is much more to cocoa bean processing than most people would expect!

The factory is currently reaping the benefits of the major investment which doubled its processing capacity and is now internationally recognised as one of the largest and most up-to-date in Europe. As part of its commitment to Hull, and the maintenance of the finest hygiene and production standards, A.D.M Cocoa Hull Ltd. will continue to invest in its technical and human resources. The founding partners of the business would have been impressed with the progress made so far.

Above: Staff in the General Laboratory in the 1950s.
Below: Two of ADM Cocoa's fleet of lorries at Hull Docks where cocoa products are exported worldwide.

new ownership. Two years later the plant was sold to Archer Daniels Midland of Decatur, USA and a further name change took place to ADM Cocoa Hull Ltd.

The capacity of the present site on Cleveland Street has almost doubled in the 1990s, with investment in buildings and plant costing in excess of £11 million. It now stretches to six acres and represents a major vote of confidence in the 'Hull' plant.

ADM is the only specialist manufacturer of cocoa products in the UK. It is a major supplier to the British chocolate and confectionery industries, making cocoa butter, cocoa powder and cocoa liquor which are also exported throughout the world.

Throughout the changes of structure, ownership and names the company has never lost sight of the reason for its half-century of commercial success - the quality of products consistently turned out by the skilled and dedicated Hull workforce. Beans coming into the factory have been meticulously selected, not only for high quality but also for particular blends which determine both the colour and flavour of the end product. On delivery to Hull, the first production process is cleaning and destoning the beans. Then they undergo one of two different processes.

To produce cocoa liquor the beans are

Hull College - education for the future

Everyone in Hull has memories of Hull College, either as a past or present student or member of staff. Hull College, founded in 1893 as Kingston Upon Hull Municipal Technical School; which by 1898 had acquired its own premises in the former Port of Hull Society's orphanage in Park Street, was renamed the Hull Municipal Technical College in 1909.

By the 1950s the 'Old Tech', as it was affectionately known by many of its students, had started a new term in its history as the Kingston Upon Hull College of Technology. A new site for the College had been found at the east end of Queen's Gardens

Courses now available at Queen's Gardens include Engineering, Hospitality, Information Technology, Health and Community Care and Building Studies. On site facilities include Construction Workshops, a Training Office, Hairdressing and Beauty Therapy suites and the Bridge Restaurant.

At the Riley Centre facilities include a 200 seater Theatre, Recording Studios, Motor Vehicle and Fabrication workshops, Multi-Gym and Design Studios. The Park Street Centre offers a wide variety of courses for adults and continuing education students, including languages, Trade Union Studies; and is the base for the extensive Community Education programme.

Hull College is now the largest provider of further and continuing education in the region and recent Further Education Funding Council inspection has confirmed its position as amongst the top twenty colleges in the country.

Above: *The Sailors Orphan Homes, originally on the site of the Park Street Centre of Hull College.*
Left: *An aerial view of the College.*
Below: *The Queen's Gardens site of Hull College.*

and the workshops there were opened in 1956. The nine storey tower block followed in 1961 and formed the major Queen's Gardens site of the Hull College of Technology.

Following reorganisation of further and higher education in Hull in the 1970s, the College became the Hull College of Further Education in 1976, with three main sites at Queen's Gardens, Park Street Centre and the Riley Centre in Parkfield Drive, which was the former Riley High School. Hull College celebrated its centenary in 1993 and the book 'A History of Further Education in Hull' was written, researched and compiled by Robert Barnard of the Local History Unit.

The grocer and tea dealer from Scale Lane

Everybody in Hull knows Jackson's: they've either worked for the firm or been a customer. It's an institution, a major food manufacturing and retailing business with a history spanning almost 150 years. Its shops occupy prime corner sites throughout Yorkshire and as far afield as the East Midlands. Its products are sold throughout Britain; it exports bread to Belgium and France, Yorkshire puddings to Canada. As a family firm in its fifth generation Jackson's is rightly proud of having adapted, diversified and re-invented itself while many of its competitors have gone to the wall.

the present site, off Derringham Street in 1907. Over the following decades the terraced houses of Victoria Street, Crystal Street and Bank Street were bought up as the firm spread its wings.

The Derringham Street factory saw the production not only of cakes, pastries and bread, but of anything from meat pies - on one famous occasion filled with crow after a shoot had been arranged around the factory yard! - to jams, pickles, bottled fruit, and even potato crisps.

The bakery side had been started by a nephew of the founder, a Mr. W. E. Cooper, but its greatest coup was the appointment, in 1896, of a volatile and talented confectioner and choco-latier John James Nathaniel Mackman. Mackman was a flamboyant man, a true artist whose creations won international recog-nition - not to mention some 5,000 cups and medals - at various trade fairs and exhibitions. "Quality not quantity" was his watchword - whatever the expense! No wonder Jackson's cakes and pastries became a must for every special occasion.

It was 1851 when William Jackson first set up as a grocer and tea trader in Scale Lane in Hull's old town, later moving to Carr Lane. It was not until 1892, after his son George had come into the business, that Jackson opened a second grocery, at 127 Spring Bank. George was keen to see the business expand, but he had other things on his mind - not least a career in politics. He stood for Parliament in the city's Central Division in 1906, but failed - despite having changed his name to Bentham to woo the Liberal vote. However, from 1910 to 1918 he represented Gainsborough.

So it was largely due to the enterprise of retail director "Bomby" Hall that the business expanded, from two branches in 1892 to fifty-plus in the early 1930s. The new shops comprised not only the tradi-tional grocery and provisions stores, but also green-groceries, butchers, a fishmonger's - and a number of bakers and confectioners.

On the back of this spectacular growth, the Company decided to develop its food production capacity. From an original bakehouse at the back of 127 Spring Bank, the firm moved its operations to

Having acquired a pork butcher's shop in 1915, Jackson's went with equal vigour into the meat trade, opening a central slaughterhouse and packing plant on Inglemire Lane, Cottingham. In the 1920s they brought in a cattle-man by the name of Harry Crawford to oversee the site. Crawford was better suited to a Wild West ranch, with his booming voice, his penchant for whisky and stetson hats. How he went down at board meetings - he became a director in 1929 - is anyone's guess.

But in any case the board was changing. With the sudden death of George Jackson Bentham in 1929, came the kind of crisis that might have destroyed a less adaptable firm. Bentham had no sons, just two daughters - Doris and Phyllis. Both girls had been courted by young officers who served at the front in the Great War, and both had married by 1919. The young men in question were brothers, Jack and Norman Oughtred. Despite their personal differ-

hundred by the 1940s, scattered through most of Yorkshire. In addition to serving the retail outlets, the firm ran a number of vans for door-to-door trade.

While the confectionery business assumed less importance over the years, bread sales continued to grow. In the 1940s Adams of Rotherham was acquired, followed by Swales of Wakefield and a number of smaller bakeries in Dudley, Harrogate and Scunthorpe. By the 1950s trade in the north of the region had reached such a level as to warrant the construction of a new bakery at Stockton-on-Tees.

ences with their father-in-law, they were both brought into the business: it was a matter of survival - and of ensuring the succession.

Over the next few years the Oughtred brothers joined the board, the extravagant Mackman left to form his own business, and the Company Secretary was shown the door - of one of H.M.'s Prisons! - after he was found guilty of "defalcations admitted and proved".

As the new branches of the business - baking, confectionery, meat and transport - made further advances, so the retail arm celebrated the opening of what was to be its flagship in Paragon Street. Staff who worked in this elegant establishment were

In the 1960s enormous changes in the flour-milling and baking business saw small operators go under in their hundreds. It was a very real fear of being cut

*Opposite page: Spring Bank branch, run for a time by Mr Bentham - until he went into politics. **This page, top:** John Holmes, driver, with horse-drawn van, 1912. Some of these horses got their noses in where they weren't wanted! **Below:** A publicity shot for Burroughs Adding Machines, taken in Inglemire Lane branch, Roy Talyor behind the counter, manageress Miss Dalton seated. The customer's chair was a fixture in most shops until the coming of self-service.*

regarded by many as "demi-gods", for it was certainly a cut above a run-of-the-mill grocery. Above the shop was a restaurant, and above that a chandeliered ballroom, one of the city's most popular night-spots.

Jackson's ran its own fleet of vehicles to serve its ever-increasing number of shops - there were almost a

tional grocery store which had been the firm's mainstay. There was no chair for a customer to sit on while her bacon was sliced or her half-ounce of pickling-spice measured out, and the range of goods on offer covered a customer's every need - from lipstick to lawn-mowers.

Meanwhile the firm continued to diversify. The craftsmen and tradesmen who were primarily responsible for fitting out the shops started to operate as Jackson's Services. This branch of the business secured such a reputation for its hotel, bank and pub refurbishments in the Hull area that offers of work came in from further afield. Before long they were working on London Airport's Terminal Four - and fitting out luxury floating hotels on the Nile!

Allied to the Services division were two other branches, Catering and Transport. The caterers, like the shopfitters, found their skills very much in demand. From their Paragon Street base, they too started to take on outside work - at the great Yorkshire Show or Beverley Races. They supplied sandwiches for the old Pullman service to London from Paragon Station, bread and cooked meats for the city's leading hotels. The Company also ran a group of public houses and restaurants such as the Ferguson Fawsitt Arms in Walkington, the pub that Jack Oughtred bought so that he could have a quiet drink after a hard day's work - or so the story goes!

off from their suppliers by the "big boys" that prompted Jackson's to buy into the Goole milling firm Edward Timm and Son, cementing a working relationship which has lasted several decades.

Just as the baking scene was changing, so the retail world was undergoing a revolution in the post-war world. And Jackson's was in the vanguard of change. Always interested in new developments, the board had sent its retail director to the U.S.A. in 1945. He was so impressed by their self-service stores that within three years the company opened one of their own in Priory Road, the first of its type in the city.

After a series of experiments with "convenience stores", "self-service groceries" and a "superette", the Grafton Street shop became the first truly successful, modern-style supermarket. Takings tripled almost overnight - even though the manageress had to stand on the pavement on the first morning and coax the bemused customers through the door!

> "THE MANAGERESS HAD TO STAND ON THE PAVEMENT TO COAX THE BEMUSED CUSTOMERS THROUGH THE DOOR!"

On the back of this venture came a more startling change of style when Jacksons opened a food hall in Britain's first discount warehouse, Grandways. Grandways was revolutionary; it took on the Government over Resale Price Maintenance, the artificial protection of over-pricing. So successful was the shop that Jackson's had bought it out within months and, with the Government yielding on R.P.M., went on in the late 1960s and 70s to carve out a second retail empire under the Grandways banner. Grandways were a far cry from the tradi-

On the transport side Jackson's have long been associated with Crystal Motors. This grew out of a need to update the Company's vehicles after the war. With customary energy, the garages in Crystal Street were updated, tyre and battery depots were opened, and sales agencies acquired. Initially these were for Dennis trucks, Trojan vans and Lea Francis' hand-built cars, but the major breakthrough was the acquisition of a Ford dealership in the 1950s. In recent years the Crystal Motor Group has operated Ford dealerships in Scarborough and Harrogate as well as Nissan in Grantham and Peugeot in Grimsby.

The diversification didn't end there. In the 1960s computerisation brought another challenge, and Jackson's picked up the gauntlet yet again. Having hired some talented experts in the field the firm then allowed them to form their own company, A.I.M., which was soon winning lucrative outside contracts.

Out of the bakery division Jackson's then developed a range of frozen Yorkshire puddings under the brand name Aunt Bessie. With a series of main meals, these have been successfully marketed alongside traditional desserts like treacle pudding and spotted dick. Despite a catastrophic fire in July 1995 which all but destroyed its plant, Tryton Foods has expanded its brand leadership and market share at a rate which echoes the Company's past successes.

However, as these developments were taking place the business climate was changing. In the 1970s and 80s diversification was the rage, but more recently companies have realised the need to look after their core activities, and one of Jackson's foundation stones was the grocery shop.

It was in 1990 that Jacksons constructed a Giant Grandways Superstore on an eleven acre site at Willerby. However, as a regional company, it found itself competing on a progressively unequal footing with the massive buying power and lower costs of the major national supermarket chains which now invaded the region. In late 1992, the Grandways chain of supermarkets was subsequently sold and Jacksons reinvented itself yet again.

So, in a second retail revolution, the firm went back to its roots, developing a new concept in shopping. Jackson's Family Food Stores offers a supermarket every bit as convenient as the old corner shop, serving the needs of a local community by opening up to twenty-four hours a day.

But if this suggests a retreat, the broader picture shows a vigorous growth. The Aunt Bessie brand is making rapid inroads, with Yorkshire puddings turned out at the rate of eight million a week; Jackson's bread is supplied both locally and to national supermarket groups; the operation of Crystal Motors reflects a continued diversity of interest; and the retail arm continues to push towards a target of 100 branches for the new millennium.

Most family firms have failed by the third generation, but Jackson's is now run by the great-great-grandchildren of the grocer and tea dealer from Scale Lane. Their Yorkshire puds may be sold on the Canadian prairies and their bread on the Canary Islands, but the name of William Jackson is still associated with the shop on the corner, and the food on the table in Hull - and across the nation.

Opposite page top: Vans await their loads outside the old Victoria Street factory, Derringham Street.
Below: The new Jackson's of concept, with its now familiar turquoise livery, sits comfortably with the old inner city store fronts.

From a caring service to a complete supplier

Hull's longest established, still family owned, 'complete office equipment supplies and service centre' has been quietly growing into a substantial operation since its formation in August 1949.

Mr James Meredith started work in 1937 as an errand boy for a firm of office suppliers in Leeds on 7/6d per week. Always keen to assist in their service department he was offered the opportunity for an apprenticeship as a typewriter mechanic. Unfortunately the Second World War intervened and James spent the next 5½ years in the RAF using

Top: The founder, Mr James Meredith.
Right: Spring Bank at the turn of the century.
Below: 97-101 Spring Bank as it appeared in 1920.

his mechanical skills keeping Spitfires in the air. During though, a brief posting at Leconfield and a night out in Hull prior to departure for North Africa, James met Marjorie, a local girl from Hessle, and following the war they were married.

James though, after being demobbed, still had to finish his apprenticeship and so spent the next two years commuting from Hull to Leeds, returning only at weekends, until he was able to obtain a transfer to their Hull branch.

In 1949 James and Marjorie decided to start their own business, initially renting a one room workshop

in Wellington Street (also at 7/6d per week). Times were hard and now with a young family as well they opted to convert their front room at home into a workshop.

A BRIEF HISTORY OF THE TYPEWRITER

Concentrating mainly on the repair and service of typewriters, with Marjorie looking after the administration and the family. James gradually built up a solid reputation and client base looking after machines for companies like Reckitt and Colman; Fenners; N.E. Gas Board; Horsley Smiths, Y.E.B.; Hull City Police and Hull Corporation. Another mechanic was employed (Mr Harry Jackson) who later went on to open his own business - Jackson Carver Ltd., ironically taken over by Merediths in 1995.

In 1960 James and Marjorie bought a shop with living accommodation at 95 Spring Bank. They then began selling typewriters - mainly reconditioned as the current models - Imperial, Remington, Underwood, Royal, Barlock and Oliver, already had existing main agents. These machine sales led to a demand for ribbons, pens, paper etc. and thus their stationery department was born. With more and more imports coming into the country, James obtained an agency for the Sterling Seimag, a solid and reliable German Model, which the Hull City Police, after extensive trials and against a furore from local councillors, introduced to all their stations. Further objections from the Imperial Typewriters factory in Hull were overturned on the basis that at the time they only produced lightweight portable machines, unsuitable for use by most Police Officers.

A further main agency for Olympia was gained with the eventual introduction of electric and then electronic office machines. During this period a duplicating service was also introduced, with

Marjorie typing the stencils and James spending the evenings running off the copies. This was a forerunner to the present day printing service, of anything from a business card to a full colour brochure.

On leaving school, James' son Don entered the business and after an initial period in the service department he gradually developed the move into furniture sales, culminating in the setting up of a second company, Kingsbridge Office Furniture Ltd. run by Don's wife Ayline. Kingsbridge now manufactures for supply locally, nationally and internationally, several ranges of contract and executive office furniture products. Meredith Business Equipment Centre can now supply a full turn-key contract from carpets to ceilings including curtains, decorating, furniture, machines and supplies.

More recent developments have taken the company into the exciting world of Web-site design and production.

Now approaching their 50th anniversary, with James and Marjorie still 'popping-in' most weeks, the company is planning a major move to a purpose built new Headquarters and looking forward to servicing their customers needs for many more years to come.

*Above: The Olympia SG 1 - the office typewriter for faster typing, popular in the 1950s. **Top right:** One of the small fleet of company delivery vehicles in the early 70s. **Top left:** A brochure telling the history of the typewriter.*

Hull Fair in the Walton Street area, taken in 1956.

First published in Great Britain by True North Books
Dean Clough
Halifax HX3 5AX
1998

© TRUE NORTH HOLDINGS

ISBN 1 900 463 86 5

COVER DESIGN/PHOTOGRAPHS COMPILED BY MARK SMITH
CAPTIONS COMPILED BY PHIL HOLLAND AND PAULINE BELL
TEXT PAGES DESIGNED BY MANDY WALKER AND NICKY BRIGHTON
LOCAL BUSINESS CONTENT ORGANISED BY STUART GLENHOLMES